ARMENIAN
ILLUMINATED
GOSPEL-BOOKS

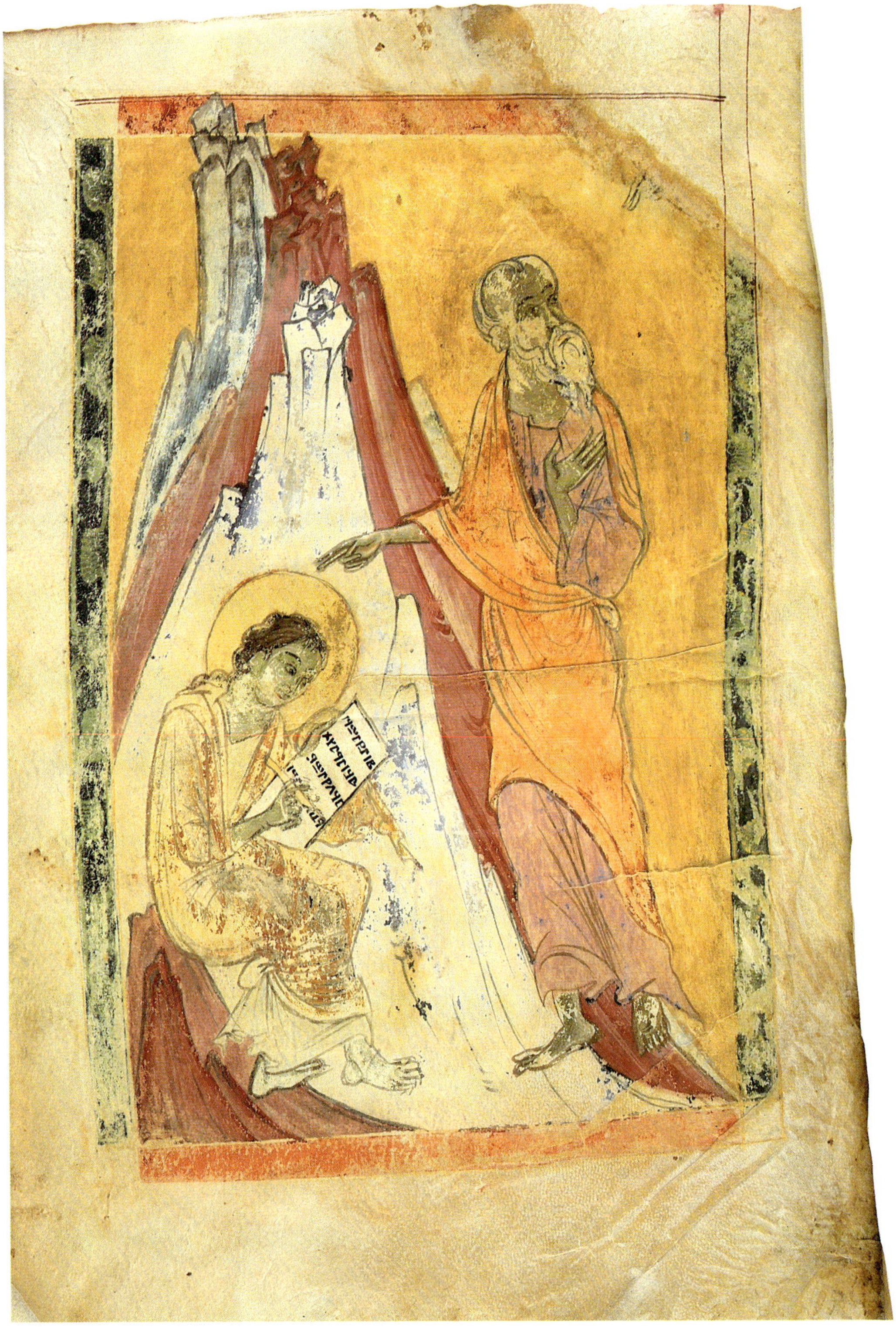

Portrait of St John and Prochorus. British Library MS Or. 5304, fol.56b.

Armenian Illuminated Gospel-Books

V. Nersessian

THE BRITISH LIBRARY

The British Library gratefully acknowledges
the assistance of the Calouste Gulbenkian Foundation
in the publication of this book.

Published on the occasion of an exhibition of the
same title at the British Library, 11 December 1987–6 March 1988

First published 1987 by
The British Library
Great Russell Street
London WC1B 3DG
and
27 South Main Street
Wolfeboro, New Hampshire
03894-2069, USA

British Library Cataloguing in Publication Data

Nersessian, Vrej
Armenian illuminated Gospel books.
1. Bible. N.T. Gospels—Catalogs
2. Illumination of books and manuscripts,
Armenian—Catalogs
I. Title II. British Library
015.566'2031 ND3073.6.A7

ISBN 0-7123-0135-6

Designed by John Mitchell
Typeset in Poliphilus and
Printed in England by
BAS Printers Limited, Over Wallop, Hampshire

CONTENTS

ILLUSTRATIONS

COLOUR PLATES *following page 53*

FIGURES

To

Leyla, Tiran and Zhirayr

PREFACE

Manuscripts from the Christian Orient (written in Syriac, Coptic, Ethiopic, and Armenian) constitute a major centre of excellence in the context of the British Library's Oriental Collections. The Christian Churches of the Middle East, dependent on the sacred narrative of the Scriptures as reflected in the Gospels, have always given equal importance to text and illustration. Within this ambience there developed distinctive artistic styles which combine Hellenistic, Byzantine and Near Eastern non-Christian traditions. But whereas the architecture of the eastern Churches has been the subject of much fruitful research, manuscript illumination as such has received more scanty attention.

Armenian illustrated manuscripts constitute one of the most important groups of codices produced by the eastern churches, both in relation to their artistic quality and as far as the number of surviving examples is concerned. Despite changing fortunes, periodic persecutions and wars suffered by the Armenian people some 26,000 manuscripts have survived covering a period from the 9th to the early 18th century; the most important collection being those of Erevan (13,836 items), Jerusalem (4,500 items), Venice (4,300 items) and Vienna (2,000 items).

Though less numerous, the British Library collection is highly representative and includes many rare and early items. Some of the manuscripts were already part of the (British Museum) Foundation Collections, others were acquired during the 19th and the earlier part of the 20th century by purchase, bequest and donation. Dr Nersessian's book will not only introduce the collection to a much wider audience but also fill an important gap in our knowledge of Armenian Gospel illustration as such. Dr Nersessian is in charge of the British Library's Christian Middle East collections and has for many years worked on this and on related subjects. The present book, which will be accompanied by an exhibition, is but one in a long list of similar research projects which include work on an exhibition and a catalogue presenting the *Christian Orient* and a *Union catalogue of Armenian manuscripts in the United Kingdom libraries and institutions* which will be published with the assistance of the Calouste Gulbenkian Foundation.

ALBERTINE GAUR
Deputy Director
Oriental Collections
The British Library
February 1987

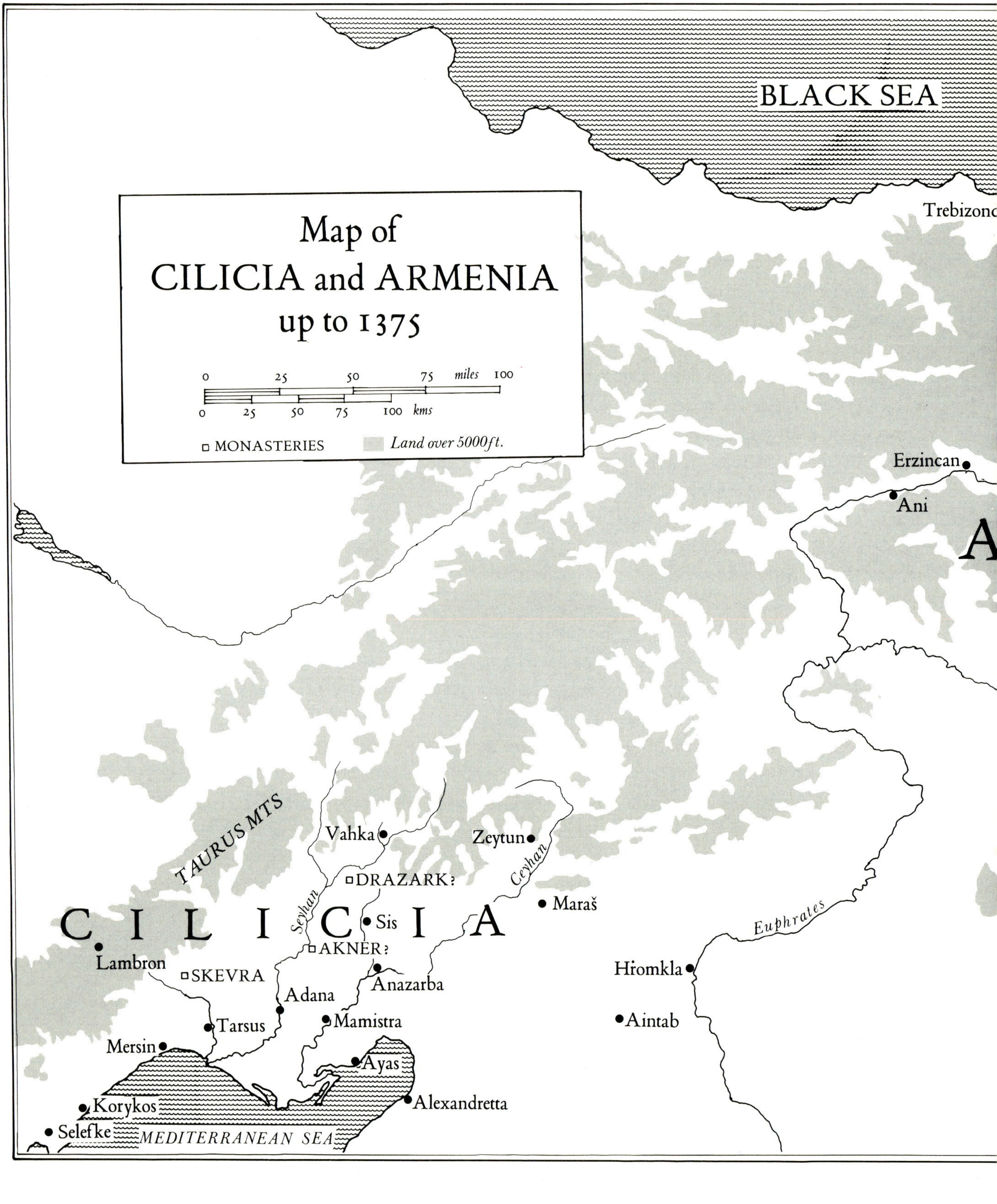

Map of
CILICIA and ARMENIA
up to 1375
0 25 50 75 miles 100
0 25 50 75 100 kms
MONASTERIES
Land over 5000ft.
BLACK SEA
Trebizond
Erzincan
Ani
A
TAURUS MTS
Vahka
Zeytun
DRAZARK?
Ceyhan
Maraš
Seyhan
C I L I C I A
Sis
AKNER?
Lambron
SKEVRA
Adana
Anazarba
Tarsus
Mamistra
Mersin
Ayas
Korykos
Alexandretta
Selefke
MEDITERRANEAN SEA
Euphrates
Hṙomkla
Aintab

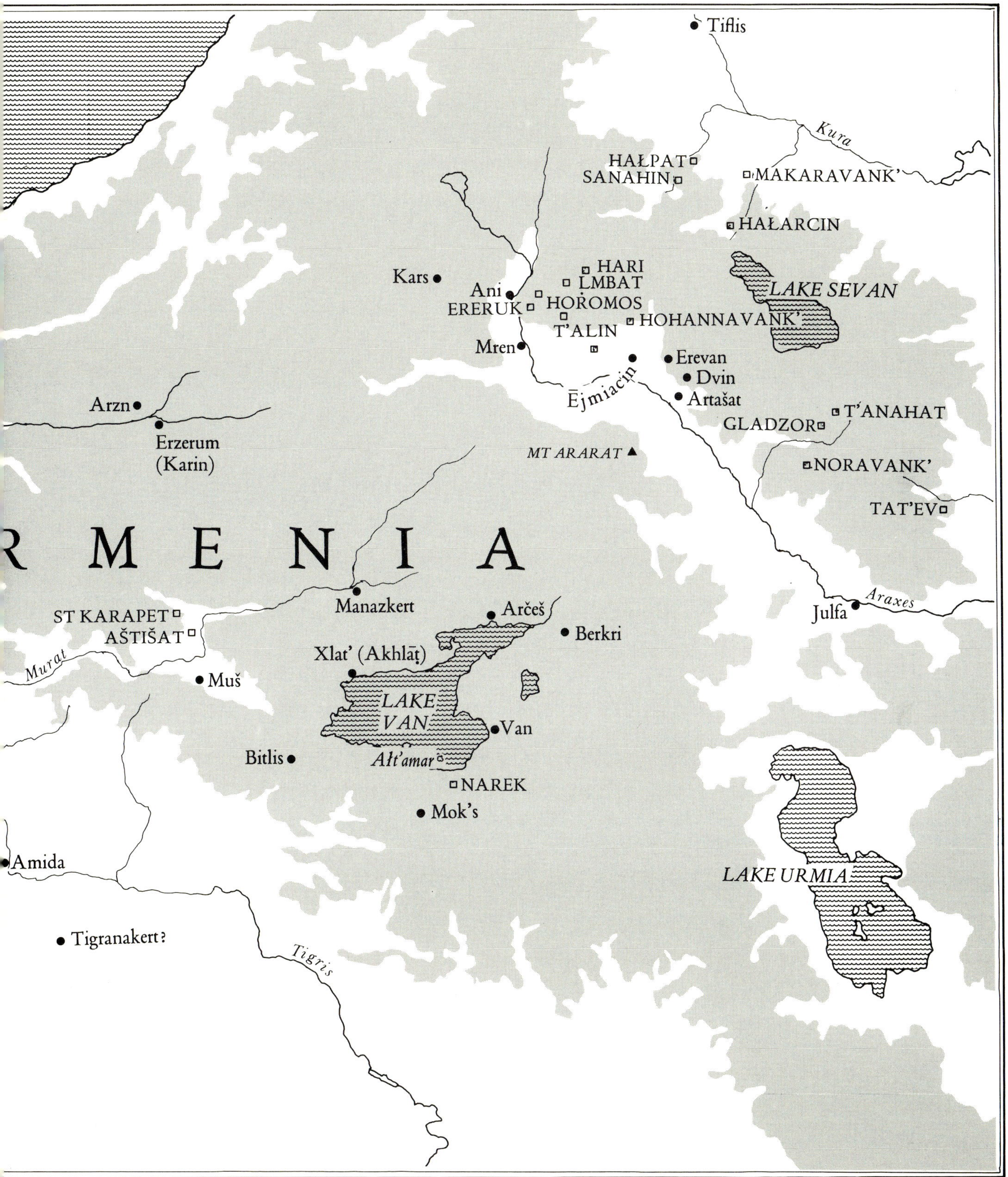

Tiflis
Kura
HAŁPAT
SANAHIN
MAKARAVANK'
HAŁARCIN
HARI
LMBAT
HOṘOMOS
Kars
Ani
ERERUK
T'ALIN
HOHANNAVANK'
LAKE SEVAN
Mren
Erevan
Dvin
Ējmiacin
Artašat
T'ANAHAT
GLADZOR
Arzn
Erzerum
(Karin)
MT ARARAT
NORAVANK'
TAT'EV
RMENIA
Manazkert
Julfa
Araxes
ST KARAPET
AŠTIŠAT
Arčeš
Berkri
Xlat' (Akhlāṭ)
Murat
Muš
LAKE VAN
Van
Bitlis
Ałt'amar
NAREK
Mok's
Amida
LAKE URMIA
Tigranakert?
Tigris

INTRODUCTION

The dependence of early Christian art on the sacred narrative embodied in the Scriptures distinguished it from the art of the pagan world and set its form and content. Whereas the Greeks and Romans possessed no all-embracing text, Christians had the Bible, the record of man's tenure on earth from the Creation to the Second Coming, which established the nature of his relation to God. Themes drawn from the Bible were illustrated in many media – fresco, mosaic, ceramic, ivory, metal, wood, textile, stone, and, most characteristically perhaps, the illuminated manuscript.

From a very early date painters collaborated with scribes in the production of manuscripts, especially in the copying of scriptural manuscripts, in which the illustrations were held to be almost as important as the sacred text itself. A century of the Christian era was to pass before the Christians overcame their dislike of the representational arts and began to make use of the formal vocabulary of classical art to teach '. . . the mystery of God, and of the Father, and of the Christ in whom are hidden all the treasures of wisdom and knowledge' (*Colossians 2:2-3*). Ultimately the church fathers not only reversed the iconoclastic attitude of the first generations of Christians, but elevated the representational arts to the highest level – that of the Scripture itself. 'The image is a memorial, just what words are to a listing ear', said John of Damascus (*c.*675–*c.*749). The earliest Christian art, that of the Roman catacombs, is symbolic. Artists decorated the catacombs with the image of an anchor, suggesting 'hope' as expressed in the Epistle to the Hebrews ('We have this as a sure and steadfast anchor of the soul' (*6:19*)), or a dove, symbol of divine wisdom and of gentleness, as indicated by St Matthew ('wise as serpents and innocent as doves' (*10:16*)). Another emblem regularly found is the fish, which served to recall the feeding of the five thousand and the sacrament of the Eucharist by the Lord, who is referred to, in the second century, as 'the huge, pure Fish from the fountain which faith provides as food'. When Christianity, in about the third century, began to use the representational arts for teaching purposes, it developed a repertory unmatched in richness and variety by any other ancient culture. The Holy Scripture, which was central to Christian life, was copied and distributed, illustrated with extensive picture cycles. The method was not new; such picture cycles had been developed centuries before for the illustration of the great classics, such as the works of Homer and Euripides, and fully developed Old Testament illustrations existed in Jewish art. The sarcophagi of the third century had carvings on them conveying the message of death, resurrection and salvation; the figures of the Good shepherd, Daniel, Noah, Jonah, Lazarus, the young men in the fiery furnace, for example, were such symbols.[1]

The crucial turning point for the Christians of the Later Roman Empire was Constantine's victory over Maxentius at the battle of the Milvian Bridge in 312, and his sudden conversion to the faith. This led to the Tolerance Edict of Milan in 313, the establishment of the Christian church as the state religion, and the birth of monumental Christian art. While Rome was at first the leading centre of the arts, it was not the only one. The cities of Alexandria and Antioch also played major roles, because, along with Rome, they assumed great ecclesiastical power as patriarchates. Later were added Constantinople (in 381) and Jerusalem (in 451). Basilicas were built in these five patriarchates, and frescoes and mosaics depicting biblical stories adorned their walls. Nilus of Sinia, in about 430, laid down the rule that churches should never be decorated with such pictures as hunting scenes, but that incidents drawn from the Old and New Testaments should appear, so that those unable to read might gain instruction. The pictorial cycles displayed publicly in this way were echoed by the illustrations in manuscripts.

GOSPEL-BOOKS

Complete Bibles do not provide the richest sources of biblical illustration. Extensive sets of pictures are found in copies of a single book or group of books, such as Genesis, or the Pentateuch. Books which contain drama and action would naturally provide more illustrative material than the others. Unquestionably the most sumptous manuscripts of any part of the Bible illustrated up to the Middle Ages were the copies of the Four Gospels bound in a single volume, frequently with splendid covers of ivory and metalwork. The Gospels were regarded with particular veneration by the faithful; an eighth-century author compared the entry of the Gospel-book at Mass during the Lesser Entrance to the entry of Christ himself. Gospel-books were also produced to be displayed on the altar, as the focal point of the service. Long cycles of illustrations to the Gospels were certainly known to Greek, Latin, and Syriac Christians by the sixth century, although the manuscripts that have been preserved, such as the Gospel of Rossano (Rossano Cathedral) and the Gospel of Rabula (Florence, Laurenziana Cod.Plut.I,56), have only a limited number of miniatures. However, the full scope of Gospel illustration becomes evident only in the manuscripts of the tenth and eleventh centuries. Two Gospel-books of the eleventh century in Florence and Paris (Laurenziana Cod. Plut.VI.23; Bibliothèque Nationale Cod.gr.74) have approximately 750 and 500 illustrations respectively. Patriarch Nichephoros (806–815), when commenting on such prolifically illustrated manuscripts, refers to the 'spoken word' and the 'painted word', the painting giving a parallel account to that of the text.

The contents of the Gospel-books are fairly uniform.[2] An important decorative feature is formed by the canon tables, ascribed to Eusebius, bishop of Caesarea (*c.*260–*c.*340).[3] These tables were designed to show which passages in each of the individual Gospels were in agreement with any of the other three. They are arranged in columns of figures under decorative arches, sometimes of great elaboration, and occasionally accompanied by scenes or symbols of the evangelists. They are to be found in all traditions.

Before each Gospel is a miniature of the respective evangelist, who is usually shown seated, though he may in some cases be represented standing. Incorporated into the portraits are the symbols of the evangelists. The setting in which the evangelists are depicted is in the form of an elaborate architectural structure. They are usually provided with a desk, a lectern and writing paraphernalia. To judge from their pose and general appearance these figures are derived from representations of ancient philosophers and poets.[4]

The early practice in Greek manuscripts was to insert frameless illustrations whenever the text required them, at the beginning of the pericope, or lection. It was the tradition of narrative illustration to have the picture physically connected as closely as possible with the text illustrated, and there was a natural tendency to represent a scene related to the very first verse of the text. Perhaps so as not to distract the Gospel reader, at an early stage of development the picture was taken out of the writing column and placed either in the margin or assembled at the beginning of the individual books.[5]

THE ARMENIAN CHURCH

Of the three major East Christian, non-Chalcedonian, churches – Coptic, Armenian, Syrian, representing three distinct geographical areas – Armenia had the least direct contact with classical civilisation. Nevertheless, it was clearly exposed to various aspects of the classical tradition, either directly, through contact with the centres of the Hellenistic world, or indirectly by way of the Greek Christian areas within the Byzantine Empire, both the capital Constantinople and the major cities in Syria and Palestine.[6]

The origin of Christianity in Armenia has always been a matter of acute controversy. This is not surprising, for there was no literature in the Armenian language during the first four centuries and therefore we have no contemporary written sources. The rapid advance of the Christian faith in Armenia in the second and third centuries paved the way for national acceptance of Christianity as the official religion at the end of the third century (287 or 289) or the beginning of the fourth century (301).

The role played by the Church throughout Armenia's turbulent history cannot be sufficiently stressed. Bulwark of Armenian language and culture, the Church was also one of the centres of resistance against all attempts at fusion or absorption. After the war that had flared up between Byzantium, heir to Rome, and Persia, peace was restored at the expense of the Armenians. The treaty of 387 divided the country on a line which ran from Erzerum in the north to Martyropolis in the south. As a consequence, the greater part of historical Armenia became a Persian dependency and remained so until a second division, in 591, favoured by Byzantium. This time the demarcation line followed the Azat river and, running to the west of Dvin and Maku, stopped at Lake Van. After the year 373 open canonical ties with Caesarea were severed, by which time the national church had become sufficiently mature and strong. The national consciousness aroused by the conversion to Christianity was reinforced in the early fifth century by the invention of the Armenian alphabet. When the fourth ecumenical council met in Chalcedon in 451 – the Armenian church recognises the doctrinal and canonical validity of the first three ecumenical councils, of Nicea (325), Constantinople (381) and Ephesus (431) as adequate for 'the basis of life and guide to the path leading to God' – Armenia was beset by very serious troubles which threatened even the existence of the Christian church. In 449 the Persian king Yazdgerd II immediately after his accession sent a letter commanding his subjects of Persian Armenia to accept Mazdaeism as their religion. This led to a general revolt by the church, the nobility and the people, led by Vardan Mamikonian. The decisive battle was waged in the plain of Avarayr, on 26 May 451. In spite of the defeat, in spite of the cruel repression and the persecution which raged for over thirty years, the Persians were unable to enforce Mazdaeism in Armenia; they finally relented and in 484 the Sassanian ruler proclaimed the freedom of religious worship.

The Arab invasions of Armenia in 640, 642/3 and 650 further complicated the political situation. In 652 the Armenian general Theodore Ṙštuni concluded a treaty with the Caliphs, recognising his suzerainty over Armenia. All Byzantine efforts to regain control over Armenia were unsuccessful and the hold of the Arabs was tempered by internal dissensions and increasing inability to control their own far-flung empire. The Armenians were not long in taking advantage of the altered circumstances. The power and prestige gained by the elder line of the Bagratuni family that began in 806, culminated in 862, when the caliph appointed Ašot Bagratuni 'Prince of princes of Armenia' and in 886 the nephew and namesake of Ašot was raised to royal dignity. The following year the emperor Basil I, himself of Armenian origin, also sent Ašot a crown. Thus the Armenian monarchy was restored after a lapse of more than four centuries.

This period of Armenian history (862–1064) marked the apogee of material prosperity and cultural revival in Armenia. After the death of Gagik I (989–1020) the Armenian Bagratuni monarchy rapidly declined due to internal rivalries and with the desire of the Byzantine emperors to expand their borders in the west; while in the east the raids of Seljuk Turks became more intensive. After the Byzantine disaster in Manazkert in 1075, Seljuk rule was firmly established in Armenia. The aftermath of the Seljuk conquest of Armenia was mass dispersion of its intellectual and political elite to foreign lands.

The most important migration of Armenians was toward south-eastern Anatolia and in 1198 a new Armenian kingdom was established in Cilicia. This opened a new chapter in the history of the Armenian people. The Crusades affected the destiny of the Cilician kingdom. Later the Mongols, on whom the Armenian kings had relied throughout in their struggle against the Sultan of Egypt, were converted to Islam, which meant that Armenia lost its ally. In 1375 the capital of Sis fell to the Egyptian Arabs and the last Armenian King Leo V was taken as a captive to Egypt.

The destiny of the Armenian nation after the establishment of the Ottoman empire on the ruins of the Byzantine dominion in 1453 was an unhappy one. The Turco-Persian wars in the seventeenth century were particularly destructive. The Persian king Shah 'Abbas (1587–1629) forced tens of thousands of Armenians to settle in the suburbs of his new capital Isfahān in 1604–5. However, a cultural centre was created here which, in its turn, through trade became one of the most important, dynamic and influential centres in the growth of the seventeenth-century Armenian cultural renaissance, both in Armenia itself and among the Armenian communities scattered all over the world but more especially in the Crimea, Syria, Constantinople, Europe and the Far East.

THE ARMENIAN BIBLE

The earliest Armenian literature, including the translation of the Bible, dates from the early part of the fifth century. The translation of the Bible is attributed to St Mesrop Maštocʿ (*c.*361–440), priest and inventor of the Armenian alphabet in 406, and the patriarch Sahak (*c.*350–439). The first book of Holy Scripture translated into Armenian was Proverbs. By 414 the Bible, practically in its entirety, seems to have been translated into Armenian. This first translation was later improved. Several books such as I and II Chronicles, I and II Macabees, Canticle of Canticles, and Sirach, have been preserved both in the original translation and in improved editions. After 436 the second translation was itself revised by Eznik Kołbacʿi and Sahak on the basis of new manuscripts brought from Constantinople. The first Armenian version of the Gospels and Acts appears to be based on a Syriac model; it seems probable that the earliest version of the Gospels was a translation of Tatian's Diatessaron. The second version, although based on the Greek, has retained some elements of the first edition. The Gospels of this version are of the Caesarean type of text. The Armenian translation displays remarkable literary qualities, combining intelligent and flexible accuracy with a respect for the genius of the language and the shades of meaning that modify words in context. It has rightly been called 'the queen of versions.'[7]

It is significant to underline the fact that it was in New Julfa that for the first time in Armenian history the idea of printing the whole Bible in an Armenian version was given serious thought. However, the technical means available at the Armenian printing press in New Julfa set up in 1636 were insufficient for such a huge and demanding project, and the attempt proved unsuccessful. But the idea was taken up by Oskan *vardapet*, who with the support of the Catholicos of the time, Hakob IV Jułayecʿi (1655–1680), and with the help of Armenian merchants from New Julfa, had the whole Bible printed in Amsterdam in 1666.

THE ORIGINS OF ARMENIAN MINIATURES

The illumination of manuscripts in Armenia must have started soon after the invention of the Armenian alphabet, but the first stages of its history – from the fifth to the eighth centuries – remain unclear because no illuminated manuscripts have survived. However, from the second half of the ninth century to the eighteenth, we can follow its development almost without interruption.

In a treatise called *Yałags Patkeramarticʿ*,[8] directed against the Armenian sects opposing the representation of images in churches, the author Vrtʿanēs Kʿertʿoł (604–607), defending the practices of the Armenian Church, enumerates the figures adorning the interior of Armenian churches; the Holy Virgin with the infant Jesus, St Grigor the Enlightener in the different stages of his martyrdom, St Stephen the protomartyr amidst his stoners, and the portraits of Saints Gayanē and Hṙipʿsimē with all their companions. In addition he also mentions scenes painted on the church walls which were inspired by the life and miracles of Jesus: 'all the wonders of Christ that are related in the Scriptures we see painted in the churches of God; the Nativity, Baptism, Passion, and Crucifixion, the Entombment, Resurrection, and Ascension into Heaven'. The mention of the purely Armenian saints makes it clear that he has in mind Armenian churches.

The authorship of Vrtʿanēs has been questioned by some,[9] on the grounds that such a treatise could not have been written before the iconoclastic controversy of the eighth and ninth centuries. However, iconoclastic tendencies were present in the Armenian church before that time. The Treatise of Vrtʿanēs was directed at the Paulicians who were rejecting the worship of images. In defending the cult of images against the heretics who considered pigments vile, Vrtʿanēs says: 'All that we find in God's Church is made from the materials of Nature, which is not to be scorned. Just as the holy writings are made of pigment, a product of Nature, so the paintings which adorn the churches of God are made with pigments too. For whatever the ear hears in church, the eye perceives in the holy figures, painted with pigment or colours. Moreover, the faithful do not worship the pigments, but Him who is represented by them.'

No surviving monument from this period has preserved the whole, or even part, of this cycle of scenes described by Vrtʿanēs Kʿertʿoł. The only Armenian church which has retained, almost in its entirety, its painted decorations is the church of the Holy Cross, built by the architect Manuēl between 915 and 921 on the island of Ałtʿamar; this enables us to study not only church decoration during the middle ages but also the style and content of Armenian iconography. In addition to the several Old and New Testament scenes which serve to illustrate the parallelism of the Old and New Testaments – the terrestial paradise lost through the Fall and regained through the Incarnation and the Sacrifice of Christ – is an extensive Gospel cycle, including minor episodes, from the Annunciation through to the Second Coming of Christ. The cycle begins on the south side and is developed on three registers around the church with hardly any break between the individual scenes, interrupted only by the niches and by the windows. The Gospel cycle includes the following episodes of the life of Christ:

The Annunciation
The Visitation
The Nativity
Joseph's dream
Flight into Egypt
The Massacre of the Innocents
The Baptism
The Transfiguration
Marriage at Cana
[*The Passion cycle*]
The Raising of Lazarus
The Entry into Jerusalem
Supper at the house of Lazarus (St John 12:1-3)
Washing of the feet
Christ before Pilate
The Crucifixion
Holy women at the sepulchre
The Harrowing of hell
Christ appearing to Mary Magdalene and the other Mary (St Matthew 28:9)
The Ascension
Pentecost
Dormition of the Virgin
Christ's Second Coming

THE EARLIEST SURVIVING ARMENIAN ILLUMINATIONS

In the same treatise *Yałags Patkeramarticʿ*, Vrtʿanēs Kʿertʿoł speaks of the sumptuous Gospels which were to be found in Armenia: 'We also see the book of the Gospels painted, and bound not only with gold and silver but with ivory and purple parchment'. The author is referring to the Greek manuscripts brought to Armenia from Constantinople for use by the translators of the fifth and sixth centuries. From what we know of the major surviving purple codices – the Rossano and Sinope Gospels, and the Vienna Genesis – all are dated to the mid-sixth century. The ivory covers which actually bind the Ējmiacin Gospels today, Byzantine works of the sixth century, are probably surviving relics from Vrtʿanēs's time and provide eloquent testimony to the accuracy of his statements. Vrtʿanēs Kʿertʿoł, while refuting the heretics' interpretation of the use of images as being idolatrous, gives us evidence of the existence of miniatures in the Gospels during the period from 604 to 607. Defending the cult of holy images against the heretics, he proves that they were introduced into Armenia at the time of the preaching of the Gospel in Armenia by St Grigor the Enlightener, coming from Cappadocia, before the reign of King Pap (367–374), who is accused by the heretics of having first introduced holy images into the churches in order to restore pagan customs.

The oldest surviving Armenian illuminations, the final four miniatures of the Ējmiacin Gospels – two leaves painted on each side, stitched on a pair of stubs at the end of the text before the colophon – originated from an older manuscript. On the basis of style, Prof. S. Der Nersessian has convincingly attributed their provenance to the 'sphere of Armenian painting prior to the Arab invasion of 640'.[10] The four valuable New Testament miniatures – the Annunciation to Zachariah, Annunciation to the Virgin Mary, Adoration of the Magi, and Christ's Baptism (fols. 228, 228b, 229, 229b) – all expound pictorially the theme of New Testament revelation. The unifying theme of the four miniatures in the Ējmiacin Gospels is the feast of the Epiphany, the celebration of which on 6 January opens the Armenian church year, embracing the birth and baptism of Jesus as told in the Gospel readings selected for the occasion.[11]

A work of outstanding quality marks the resumption of artistic activity after centuries of Arab occupation; this is the Gospel known as that of Queen Mlkʿē, illustrated in 862, now one of the treasures of the Mekhitharist Congregation of Venice (MS 1141/86).[12] Queen Mlkʿē, the wife of Gagik I (*d.*1020) who was one of the owners of the manuscript, in 902 gave it to the monastery of Varag, and by 1881 it was in the Venice collection. Various scholars who have compared the miniatures of this work with those of the Rabbula Gospels of 586 are quite convinced that the model used by the painter of the Mlkʿē Gospels was a 'classicising' manuscript of a very early period. The only narrative miniature in the manuscript is a full-page picture of the Ascension which according to Mesrop Janashian was the last miniature of a cycle that probably comprised the Sacrifice of Isaac, the Annuciation, and the Baptism of Christ.

In the survey *Illuminated Armenian manuscripts to the year 1000* AD.,[13] covering the period from the sixth to the end of the tenth century, the following tabular results are obtained:

The Sacrifice of Isaac (3 miniatures)
Annunciation to the High Priest (1)

Annunciation to the Virgin (2)
Nativity limited to the Adoration of the Magi (1)
Christ's Baptism (2)
Crucifixion (1)
Ascension (1)

There are several 'symbolic' full page miniatures. Christ enthroned, flanked by two evangelists (1), Virgin and Child (3), a sanctuary representing the Holy Sepulchre (4), ornamental cross (4). Finally sixteen evangelist's portraits (of which three are half-page miniatures) are known: Matthew (2), Mark (2), Luke (2), Matthew and Mark (2), Mark and Luke (2), Luke and John (1), the four evangelists together (1).

Within the wide range of methods of Gospel illumination used in Byzantine and east Christian art, the 'classic Armenian' method constitutes a unique contribution. As represented in the manuscripts of the eleventh century, the Armenian type consists of a set of full-page scenes which follow the canon tables and which are in turn followed by portraits of the evangelists, the four often grouped together on a single page. This scheme of illustration continued to be used in Armenian manuscripts down the centuries, even though other models were known and used.

T. A. Izmailova has drawn attention[14] to four manuscripts, all dating from the first half of the eleventh century and belonging to the school of Melitene which have the most extensive cycle of pictures representing the life of Jesus Christ. The author maintains that the cycle of pictures in this group of manuscripts is liturgical and not narrative and that they were adapted from the wall-paintings of the Cappadocian churches. She compares the cycle of paintings in the church of Qaranlek with the cycle of miniatures that occur in MS 3624 of Jerusalem dated 1041 and MS 3784 of the Matenadaran dated 1057. The following picture emerges:

Qaranlek Church	*MS 3624 (AD 1041) & 3784 (AD 1057)*
1. —	Annunciation
2. Voyage to Bethlehem	—
3. Nativity	Nativity
4. —	Presentation in the Temple
5. Baptism	Baptism
6. Transfiguration	Transfiguration
7. Raising of Lazarus	Raising of Lazarus
8. Entry into Jerusalem	Entry into Jerusalem
9. The Last Supper	The Last Supper

Qaranlek Church	*MS 3624 (AD 1041) & 3784 (AD 1057)*
10. Betrayal by Judas	Betrayal by Judas
11. Crucifixion	Crucifixion
12. Entombment	—
13. Descent into Hell	Descent into Hell
14. Ascension	Ascension

The iconographical programme no doubt comprised a series of pictures depicting the major dominical feasts. In the Middle Byzantine period a set of twelve pictures had been selected in church decorations as well as in icon painting, but it must be stated that there is nothing canonical about the number twelve and the cycle can include additional feast pictures. For instance the Passion is represented in a number of additional pictures depicting the Washing of the feet, the Last Supper, and the Hearing before Pilate inserted between the Entry into Jerusalem and the Crucifixion.

THE NATURE OF IMAGE VENERATION IN ARMENIA

Armenian painting, being essentially Christian and traditional, had to represent what is intangible and imperceptible and to narrate in colour and line the events drawn from the earthly life of Jesus. The paintings were never a gratuitous act but a functional one, since the religious images were created to enable the believer to apprehend the divine and follow visually the life story of Jesus. The efficiency of the image did not depend upon realism but upon the representation of what was recognised as the principle of the things portrayed and as the thinking of the Armenian church. The spirit pervading the paintings was Christian, expressing simple and fervent feelings.

The purpose of the painting was didactic as well as intercessional and propitiatory. The Gospel story was seen not as a historical succession of isolated events, but rather as a unified whole made immediate by the sacramental re-enactment of the great mysteries of the story – the Incarnation of Christ, His teachings, His sacrifice, the miracles, and His glorification. Paintings were made to enable people to visualise the sublime drama of the Gospels, and the mysteries of the faith, and to portray the holy personages in a form intelligible to believers who could not read.

For centuries, many Christian communions and historians have accused the Armenian Church of being iconoclastic. Very often during the historical growth and development of the Church in Armenia, religious movements (for example the Paulicians and the T'ondrakians) emerged and taught an iconoclastic doctrine. It must be remembered that these were not representative of Armenian Orthodox theology and doctrine. From the earliest days of the church and then during its eventual growth in Armenia, images and icons always had an important place in the expression of the devotion and piety of the faithful. With the growth of Christianity in Armenia, icon veneration developed and became a natural expression of piety. Internally and externally the churches were adorned with images – particularly the cross, the images of Christ, the saints and also pictures of biblical events. As early as the sixth century adornment of a church was usual. The illuminated Gospels are also included within the scope of miraculous images and were themselves venerated.

The importance accorded to manuscripts by Armenians is in some respects comparable to that accorded to icons by the Greeks. Just as the Byzantine emperors sometimes carried an icon, as a *palladium*, during their military campaigns, the Armenians took with them the Holy Gospel. Manuscripts, especially those endowed with miraculous powers, were given special names, for instance 'Saviour of All', or 'Resurrector of the dead', just as special names were given to particular icons.[15] The large number of manuscripts that have survived despite the destruction wrought by time and man testifies to the important place they occupied in the lives of the people. The manuscripts were thought of as pledges for the salvation of the donors, as imperishable treasures set in heaven, and this also explains the fact that Armenian manuscripts are rarely anonymous productions. The sponsors, as well as the scribes and the painters, wished to record their names in testimony of their pious act, so that they might be recalled in the prayers of all those who had occasion to use these manuscripts.

The Church adopted this devotional piety from pagan worship, and sanctified it through Christianity by the sacrament of 'The order of consecration of painted pictures in a church'.[16] Nevertheless, it was very often looked upon as a vestige of pagan worship. Such opposition provoked Armenian church fathers to define and defend this expression of Christian piety (for example, Vrtʿanēs Kʿertʿoł, Yovhannēs Ōjnecʿi, Yovhannēs Mayragomecʿi, Łewond *vardapet*, Grigor Magistros, Nersēs Šnorhali, Grigor Tatʿevacʿi). The most precise understanding of icons and images and their purpose and place in the Armenian church and theology is expressed by Vrtʿanēs Kʿertʿoł in the following three quotations:

> 'When we bow before the Holy Gospel, or when we kiss it, we do not worship the ivory or the red paint . . ., but we worship the word of the Saviour written on the parchment.'
>
> '. . . It is not because of the colours that we prostrate ourselves before the images but because of Christ in whose name they are painted.'
>
> '. . . For we attain the invisible through what is visible and the pigments and pictures are memorials of the living God and His Servants.'[17]

This theology is summed up by the following prayer recited by the priest at the beginning of the celebration of Holy Mass: 'In the midst of this temple, and before these God-receiving and thus made resplendent holy signs, we bow down in fear and worship.'[18]

MANUSCRIPTS IN THE BRITISH LIBRARY

CILICIAN MINIATURES

The first chapter of Armenian painting comes to a close with the Seljuk invasions. Work was resumed in the new national home established in Cilicia (1080–1375).[19] The Armenian artists in Cilicia did not break off links with their native land, considering the new kingdom to be a political successor to the state of Greater Armenia. Colophons copied into Cilician manuscripts contain information about older manuscripts, brought to Cilicia from Greater Armenia, which served as both model and inspiration for the Cilician artists. The most prominent centres of art and written culture were the monasteries of Hṙomkla, Drazark, Akner, and Gṙner, located near the city of Sis and associated with the royal family; and finally, Skevra, which belonged to the domain of the Ōšin family, the most influential and enlightened of all Cilician Armenian princely houses.

Among the British Library collection of manuscripts there are four of this period. The earliest of these is Add. MS 21932, ascribed to the tenth century, written on vellum. An interesting and archaic feature of this manuscript is the fact that the text is not divided into pericopes (which were usual from about the eleventh and twelfth centuries onwards). It has no decoration. The next in the group is Add. MS 19727, which is written on glazed oriental paper, now much yellowed. The script is in neat, almost continuous, square *erkatʿagir* sloping to the right, in double columns of twenty-one lines. The history of the manuscript is complicated. There are four colophons, one of which on fol. 310b states 'have mercy on the unworthy servant, the scribe who wrote this book, in thine awesome advent, on the hidden Sunday, and glory be to thee now and unto unending aeons. Amen. It was written in the Armenian year 82'. On fol. 26 there is a brief note in *notr* (cursive) script stating 'This Holy Gospel was before [the time of] Zonan Ōjnecʿi', that is Yovhannēs III Ōjnecʿi, Catholicos from 717 to 728. F. C. Conybeare took the statement in the colophon to the 'Armenian year' as being a reference to the 'Great Armenian era' so he added 551 years, the difference between the Armenian era and the modern calendar, and arrived at the date of AD 633 which he rightly regarded as 'impossible for the volume before us cannot be older than the twelfth century'. However Revd. Baronian suggested that the scribe was using not the 'Great Armenian era' but the so called 'Lesser Armenian era' devised by Yovhannēs *Sarkawag* which began in AD 1084, and in which year 82 would be AD 1166. Several examples of the use of this dating are cited by Prof. A. G. Abrahamyan and a similar problem is found in MS 556 of the Chester Beatty collection.[20]

An illuminated headpiece precedes each of the Gospels on fols. 8a, 92a,

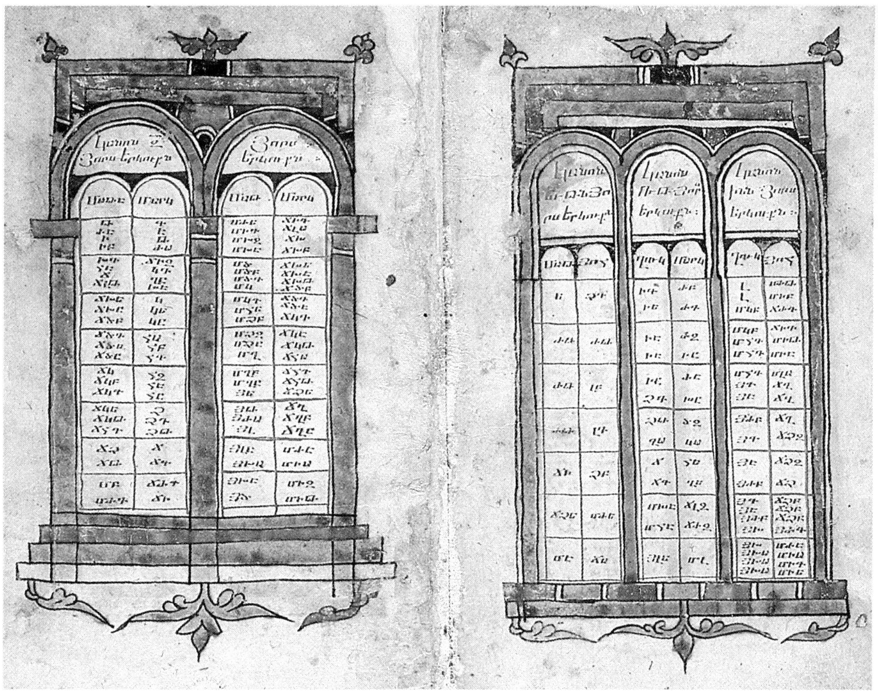

Fig. 1. *Four Gospels (Add. MS 19727). 15.5 × 10 cm. fols. 6b–7a. Canon Tables.*

147a, and 240a. St Matthew's Gospel has a '⊓'-shaped carpet headpiece in green, black, and red, decorated with six circles and quatrefoils and has a square niche – within which is the title of the Gospel 'Awetaran est Matʿēosi'. The initial letter 'G' extends to the whole length of the page, with ten lines of text in red ink on a plain background (Fig. 2). The canon tables on fols. 4a–7b (Fig. 1) are written within single or double arcades except the table on fol. 7a which has three arcades, executed in red and green. The Letter of Eusebius to Carpianus on fol. 3b has a circular arcade, the second half of which is missing because of the loss of a folio. The numbers of the chapters, or forty-two Pentecostal lections of each Gospel, are given in the margin surrounded by circles or other simple ornate designs drawn in green ink.

Cilician book painting reached its peak between 1250 and 1290. Its magnificent achievements developed from the miniature art of the preceding $1\frac{1}{2}$ centuries. The distinctive style of the Cilician miniature began to take shape towards the end of the twelfth century. Special consideration should be given to British Library MS Or.81, a Gospel book written on vellum by the scribe Tʿoros and decorated by the artist Xačʿatur in AD 1181–82, as an example of the earlier phase of Cilician painting. The main colophon on fol. 373 records that the manuscript was 'written in the monastery called Drazark by Tʿoros, by order

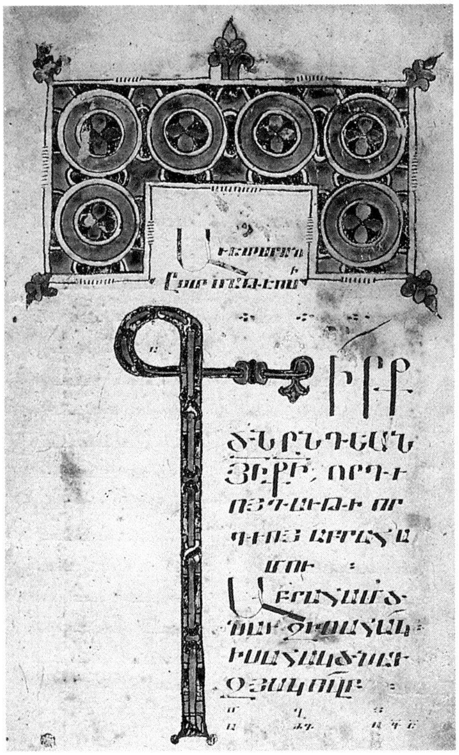

Fig. 2. *Add. MS 19727. fol. 8a. The headpiece of St Matthew's Gospel.*

of Samuēl, in the patriarchate of Tēr Grigor, Catholicos of Armenia, and in the reign over this canton of Ruben, a pious prince'. The precise date of this manuscript is established with the help of the personages named in the colophon. Tēr Grigor called *Tłay* was Catholicos between 1173–1193. Ruben II was king of Cilician Armenia between 1174–1185 and the 630th year of the reign of the Persian king Khusrau would be AD 1181.*

MS Or.81 opens with a miniature on fol. 1b of Samuēl, primate of the monastery of Drazark and owner of the manuscript, presenting it to Christ. The figures are crude in colour and design, against a blue and green background now badly soiled. Fols. 2b–3a contain the Letter of Eusebius to Carpianus and fols. 4b–7a the canon tables (fols. 3b, 4a, 5b, 6a, 7b, 8a are blank). The text of the letter and the concordance tables are contained in shallow semi-circular arches within rectangular traceried heads in blue, red and gold, with peacocks and crosses above. Each of the four Gospels is preceded by a full-page portrait of the Evangelists on fols. 8b, 111b, 180b, and 289b. On fol. 111b St Mark, bearded and with halo, is seated facing right, wearing a green gown over a white tunic. He is holding a pen in one hand and writing on a book resting on his knees, and in the other hand he is holding the book placed on a lectern on the left of the picture (PLATE I). All the evangelists are depicted seated writing, with their names inscribed above their heads. The symbols of the respective evangelists are represented neither in the portraits nor in the respective headpieces. In the case of St John (fol. 289b) Prochoros is not represented. Instead the hand of God is depicted coming out of the segment of sky as the sign of inspiration. The most attractive and accomplished features of this manuscript are the headpieces of the respective Gospels, all well executed in green, red, and gold, surmounted by birds and other decorations. Each Gospel begins with a festooned *šełagir* initial almost as tall as the page, while the rest of the letters of the text are written in large gold uncials on a blue background (PLATE I).

Two manuscripts in the British Library collection belong to the last quarter of the thirteenth century; MSS Or.5626 (AD 1282), and Or.2283 (AD 1295),

*Until recently in the discussions of this phase of Cilician history of manuscript illuminations a Gospel book in the Tübingen University Library (MA XIII) and Matenadaran MS 7737 were included as principal examples of works produced in the monastery of Drazark. However, the scholar Y. Kurdian following the lead of N. Akinian has in his article devoted to 'The Gospel of the Tübingen University and its supposed colophon of 1113' published in *Handēs Amsoreay*, 4–6 (1968), 158–163 proved beyond doubt that these two manuscripts were not copied in Drazark but in Siunikʿ in the second half of the thirteenth century. The colophon with the statement that the model was copied in AD 893 has since been recognised as a forgery.

the artistic features of which enable us to judge the progress made in the Drazark school since 1181–82.

MS Or.5626 is a manuscript of the Four Gospels copied on vellum by the scribe Barseł 'in the great era of the Armenians seven hundred and . . . in the twelfth year of the reign of King Lewon, and in the fifteenth year of the patriarchate over the Armenians of Tēr Yakob, this holy Gospel was written in the famous monastery of Drazark, under the shelter of the Mother of Light, the Theotokos, as a memorial of Tʿoros *vardapet*' (fol. 160b). The Armenian king referred to in the colophon is Leo II/III, who ascended the throne in AD 1269 and was crowned in AD 1270. His twelfth year was therefore AD 1282. Yakob I Klayecʿi became Catholicos in AD 1268 and his fifteenth year might have begun in late AD 1282. This, then, is the date of the manuscript, and the year of the Armenian era of which the second number is defective in the colophon should be read as 731.

This manuscript is richly illuminated, and gold has been lavished on it. Four full-page portraits of the evangelists (fols. 1b, 101b, 161b, 266b) precede their respective Gospels, all exceedingly well executed, particularly that of St Mark. The heads of the evangelists have gold backgrounds, but are full of life and are quite unconventional. The portrait of John and Prochoros is especially lifelike. Each Gospel begins with a coloured headpiece of interlacing fronds in blue, red, and black, on a gold ground. Harpies, gryphons, or lions are framed in the foliage. The initial letters of the texts are fashioned out of the evangelist's symbols (angel, lion, and ox) for Matthew, Mark, and Luke; and in the case of St John all the symbols of the four evangelists combine to form the letter 'I'. The remaining lines of the texts of the beginning of each Gospel are in repeated lines of gold, blue and red capitals in double columns. In the margins are tall and elegant arabesques in blue, red, and green, outlined with gold. Three different artists have contributed to the illustrations. An inscription under the portrait of St Matthew in gold uncials on blue ground reads 'Remember in Christ the sinful soul Yohanēs', who also painted the headpiece of St Matthew's Gospel (PLATE II). The portrait of St Mark belongs to a second artist and a third artist has painted the portraits of St Luke and St John. The later colophon on fol. 343b, not deciphered by Conybeare, states that the manuscript was restored in 1426 when after 'it had fallen into the hands of unbelievers . . . it was again received by the priest Martiros who presented it to the church of Holy Astuacacin at Sanahin where Yovhanēs a *spasawor* (servant) of Holy Astuacacin again restored in script (*gir*) and with flowers (*całik*)'. It is worth recalling that from 1420 this Yovhanēs is mentioned several times as one of the scribes and artists active at the monastery of Sanahin.

Another manuscript belonging to the closing decade of the thirteenth century is MS Or.2283, a very interesting manuscript which has not been sufficiently discussed. The style of decoration is typical of the work done in Greater Armenia in the monasteries of Hoṙomos, near Ani, Hałbat, in the northern part, and Hohanavank', in the province of Ayrarat. MS Or.2283 was copied by two scribes. The first half is in large irregular *bolorgir*, in double columns of twenty-one lines as far as fol. 130, and then of twenty-two lines to the end, in a less archaic style. The decoration in the section fols. 4–134 is less ornate than in the section following fol. 135 to the end. The liturgical sections in this earlier part have, as a rule, red uncials only, and in but one or two cases ornamental letters of interlacing red lines; at the beginning in the margins are crude geometrical arabesques and bosses, generally in black outline, but sometimes filled in with red pigment. The only marginal miniature, of a horse on fol. 125b, is a later addition. From fol. 135 onwards however, the lections begin with large *šełagir* or festooned initials, coloured red, green and blue; and the marginal bosses and arabesques are also more elaborate and colourful.

These two distinct styles are accounted for in the provenance of the manuscript. According to the first colophon on fol. 144 'I, a sinful servant of God, K'ahanay and Šmawon, we wrote this holy Gospel as a memorial of ourselves'. K'ahanay and Šmawon were brothers, educated and raised in the convent of T'ełenik' 'at the feet of our holy and venerable and aged father's brother Nahapet'. In the second colophon on fol. 226b the priest Šmawon records the fact that his brother K'ahanay died and he 'had the manuscript completed with much labour and zeal by David'. The third colophon in slightly smaller *bolorgir*, written by the scribe David, confirms that 'in the year of the Armenian era 744 [AD 1295] in the days of the Archers' race, that had overcome by force all the land of Armenia and many other lands whereof I cannot describe the bitterness, nor the desolation of the land, which resembles a stormy sea . . . had the manuscript completed in the monastery of T'ełenik', under the shelter of Holy Astuacacin'. David adds 'He who began it, one called by name K'ahanay . . . [had] got half through it when death surprised him and carried him off . . . However, his brother, the venerable and inspired priest Šmawon, found the Holy Gospel, and had that written out which his brother had not been able to, and it was completed by me the unworthy David'.

Each Gospel begins with a large ornamental headpiece of differing styles. The headpiece of St Matthew is a simple plain line drawing of a double interlacing arch filled with a text praising the Gospel and two columns of text of eleven and thirteen lines each. The headpieces of St Luke and St John are similar but with minor differences, and the work of a single artist. They comprise an arch of interlacing white tracery against red background. The first letter of each Gospel is a beautifully executed *šełagir* filling the whole length of the inner

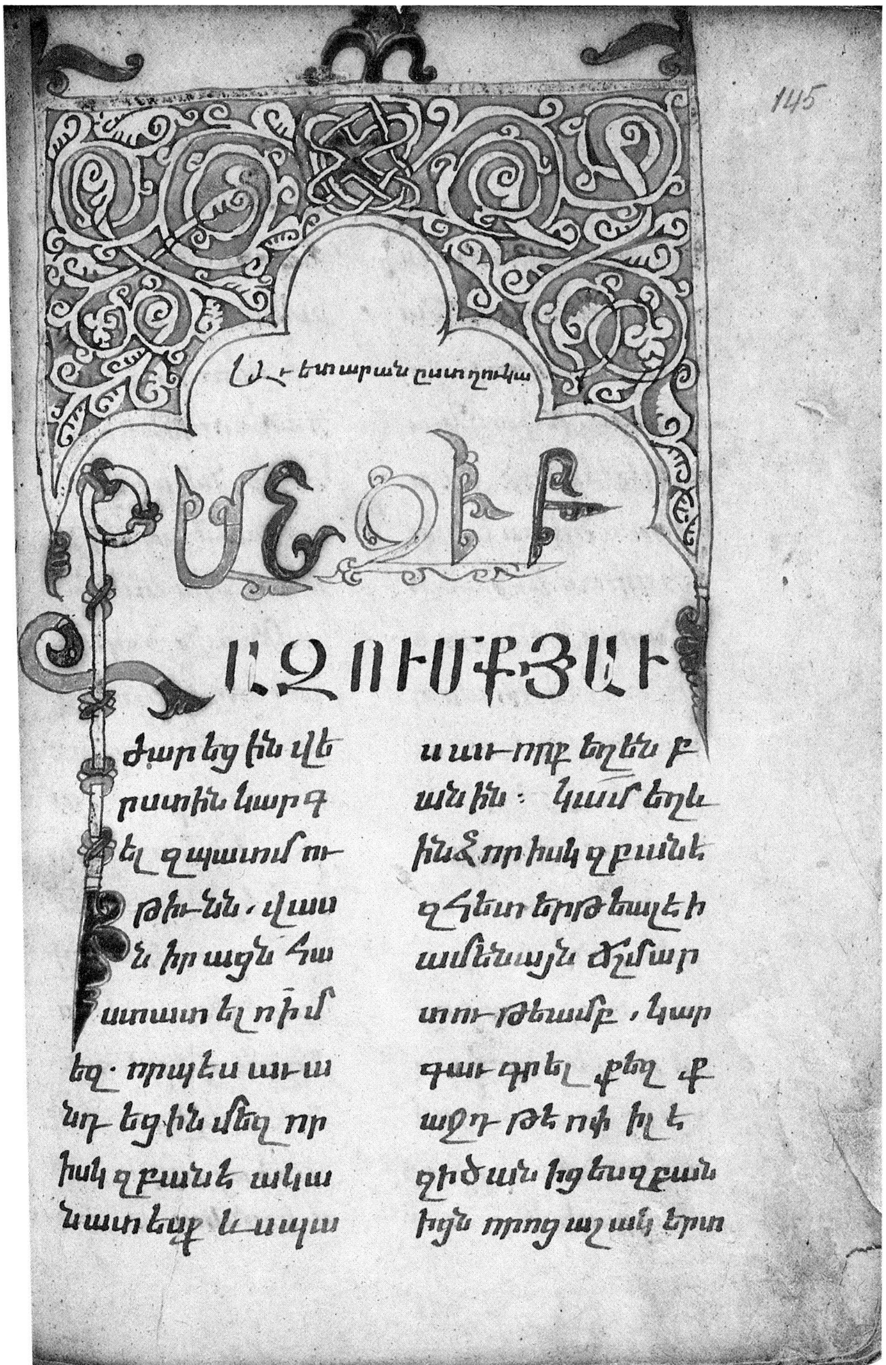

Fig. 3. *Four Gospels (MS Or.2283).*
23 × 15 cm.
fol. 145. The headpiece of St Luke's Gospel.

margin (Fig. 3). The most interesting is St Mark's headpiece (Fig. 4). It consists of a rectangle resting on two columns. The rectangle is decorated with foliage design drawn in white tracery against a red background. In the centre of the rectangle a lion holding a book, the symbol of St Mark, is drawn in a circle. Below, within the two columns, the first three letters of the word 'skizbn' are in coloured *šełagir* and the rest of the text is continued in single column of three lines in red and black ink. In the upper half of the outer margin there is an interlacing palmette supporting an ornate cross. The place assigned to the symbol of the evangelist differs from the usual practice of the artists of Greater Armenia, who represent each symbol next to the first letter of the Gospel, or fashion the initial letter out of the respective symbols.

THE AWAG VANKʿ GOSPELS

Another remarkable manuscript and probably the most important in the British Library collection is MS Or.13654, called the Awag Vankʿ Gospels, bought in 1975 and formerly belonging to the collection of the late Hagob Kevorkian of New York.[21] This manuscript, consisting of 384 vellum folios measuring 37 × 29 cm is among the largest of ancient Armenian manuscripts. The text is written in black ink in heavy majestic upright uncials in double columns, with seventeen lines per column. The principal colophon on fols. 380–383b records that the manuscript was commissioned by the bishop Tēr Sargis and his brother Ambakum, priest, as a memorial for their paternal uncle Tēr Awetik', bishop, and was completed by the scribe Vardan *dpir*, in 649 (AD 1200–1202) in the monastery of Awag Vankʿ on Mount Sepuh, eleven miles south-west of Erzindjan. The scribe Vardan is possibly the same Vardan *Kaṙnecʿi* who in 1200–1202 copied in the same monastery the Mush Homiliarum, now Erevan MS 7729. A memorial notice on fol. 2a relates the arrival of the manuscript in Constantinople with a group of refugees 'from the land of Daranałikʿ, that is Kemał' shortly after August 1605, and its presentation to the church of St Nicholas, by a certain Setʿ, son of Yakob and Kost. Some-time later, possibly in the eighteenth century, the manuscript passed into the Armenian National Library at Galata. It was catalogued as MS 6 of this collec-tion between 1902 and 1907 by its librarian, Babgen *vardapet* Kiwlesērian, the future coadjutor Catholicos of Cilicia.[22]

Apart from its historical importance, this manuscript is equally interesting for its illuminations, though some of those originally in the manuscript are now missing. The decorations of the manuscript, restricted in scope to the roundels enclosing the Letter of Eusebius (fols. 1b, 2a) (Fig. 5), the Eusebian concordance

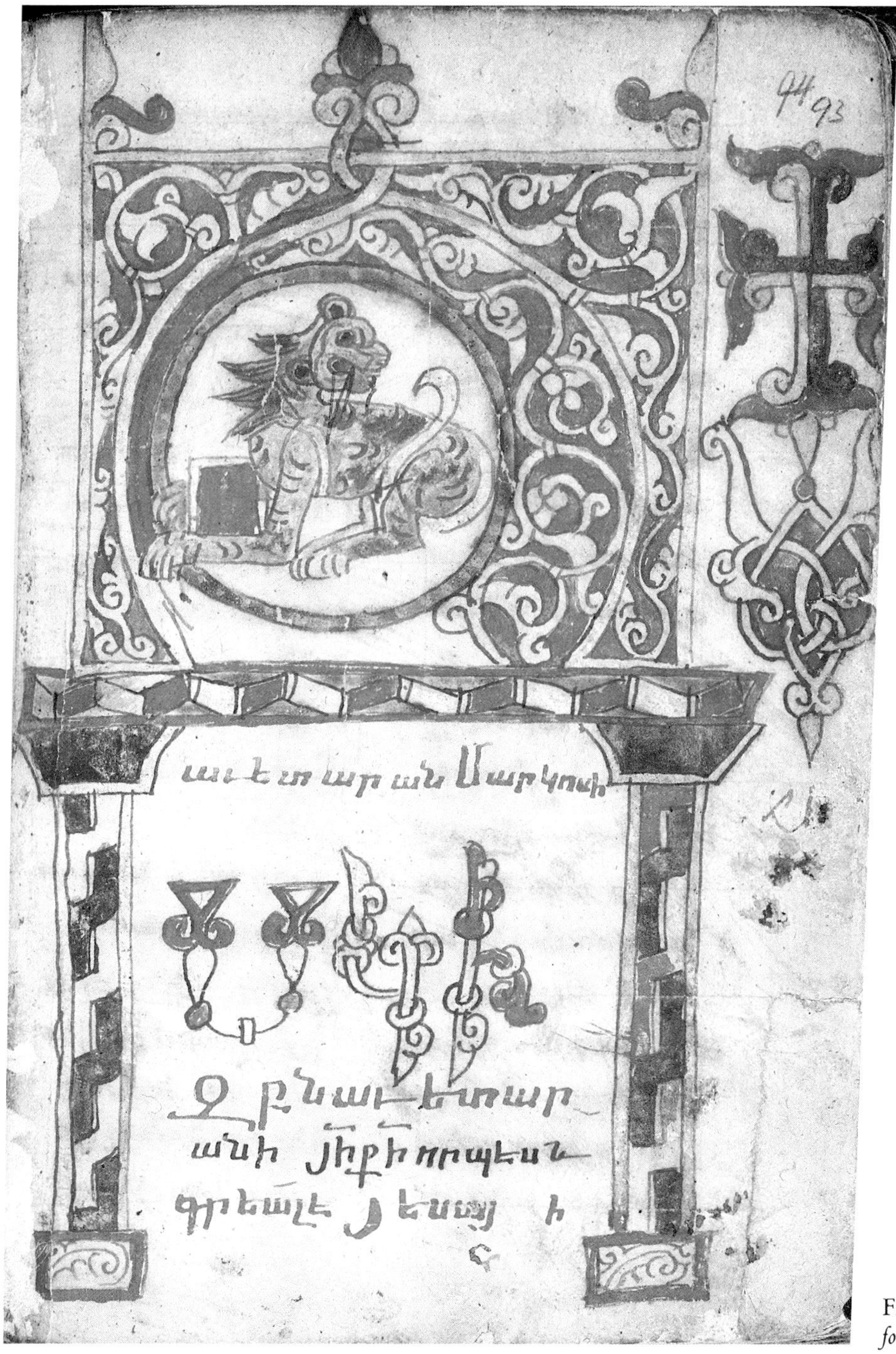

Fig. 4. *MS Or.2283.*
fol. 93b. The headpiece of St Mark's Gospel.

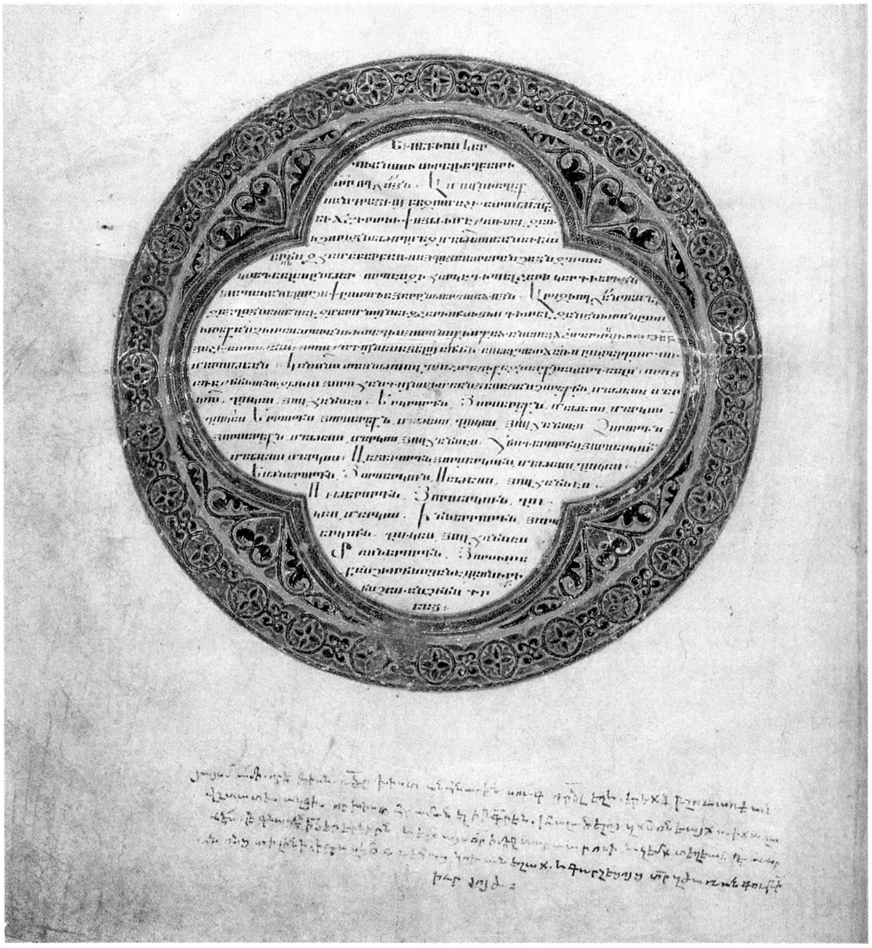

Fig. 5. *The Awag Vankʿ Gospels (MS Or.13654).*
37 × 29 cm.
*fol. 1b. The Letter of Eusebius to Carpianus. The Letter of Eusebius, instead of being written under architectural frames similar to those of the Canon Tables (*PLATE III*), is written in the quatrefoil, framed by an ornate circular band. The four-line notice in* notragir *was added to the lower margin at the beginning of 1609: 'In this year, the year 1058 [20 October 1608] severe, enormous affliction came again upon thrice wretched nation, which has seen much misery, when a severe command came from the king [Sultan Ahmed I, 1603–17] to drive us Christians from this town, saying "Go to your own country"; and we are today in the midst of Tartarus, and we do not know what the end will be. We have been trampled upon as "the mite of the streets" and the Lord has "abhorred his heritage greatly".'*

tables (fols. 3b, 4a, 5b, 6a) and the title pages of the Gospels (fols. 7a, 117a, 182a, 299a) are very finely executed in a style reminiscent of the art of Cilician Armenia, which in the year 1200 was on the threshold of its greatness, represented above all others by Tʿoros Roslin. The title pages are of traditional Cilician design with local inspiration particularly as regards to the evangelist's symbols. Each title page bears an ornate headpiece above the title, which is written in small gold uncials, supporting peacocks in various attitudes, in colours and in gold; the initial capital is a large geometrical composition. The evangelists' symbols are strikingly different in style and execution: they are in bold colour but without gold, and are naïve in conception. They are obvious afterthoughts, added to conform with another style. Whereas the lion and eagle

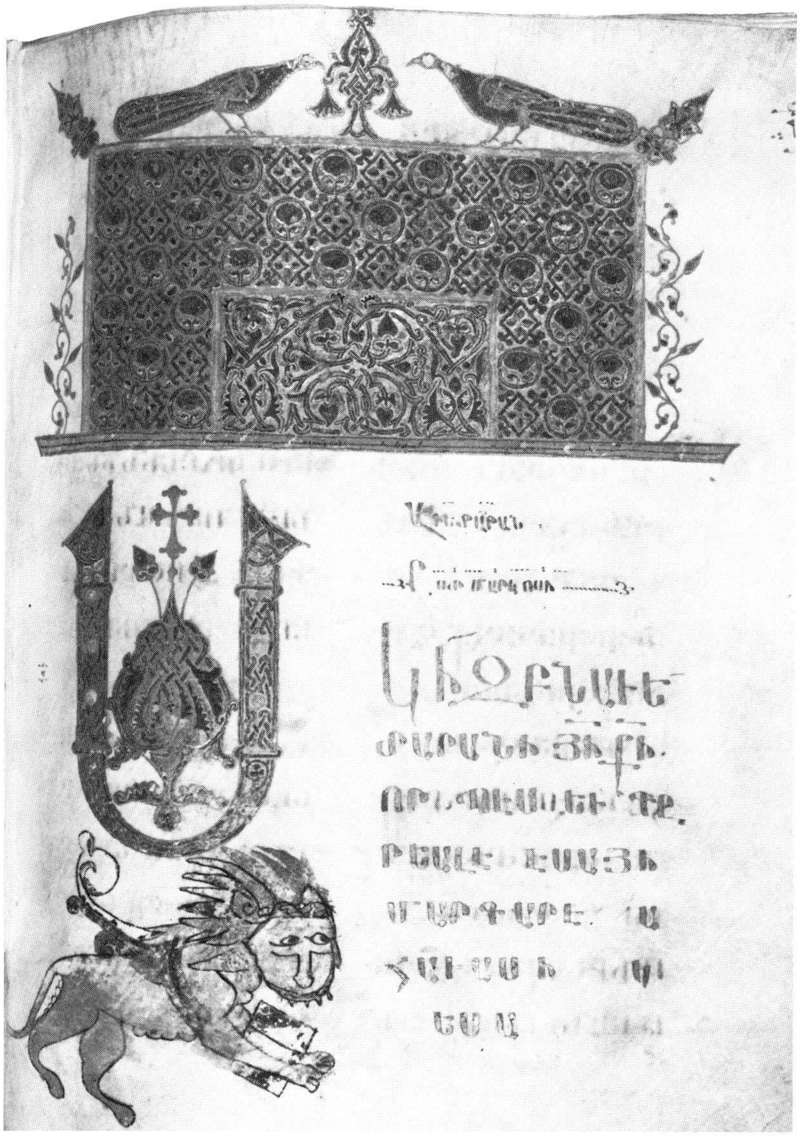

Fig. 6. *MS Or.13654. fol. 117a. The headpiece of St Mark's Gospel The large initial capital 'S' in the shape of a basket in the centre of which there is an attractive floral motif supporting a simple cross. The lion of St Mark is placed below the initial, clutching a blue book between his front legs, the edge of his far leg showing through the book evidence that the representation of the book is a later addition. In the narrow yellowish band forming the base of the headpiece the scribe has, in barely visible miniscule* bolorgir, *written 'I said in my appreciation that all men are vain'.*

of St Mark and St John are placed fairly harmoniously (Fig. 6; PLATE IV) on the page below the initial letter, Matthew's angel is awkwardly in the right-hand margin, and Luke's ox ascends the stem of the decorated initial 'K' in a manner more suited to a fly.

The scriptorium of Awag Vankʿ, in the canton of Daranałik, Kemał, both less than thirty miles from Erzindjan, was within the political and artistic sphere of influence of the city of Sis. Famous for the Erzindjan Bible of 1269, which Prof. S. Der Nersessian has called one of the masterpieces of Armenian illumination, she does not hestitate to ascribe the Awag Vankʿ Gospels to an Erzindjan school.[23]

CILICIAN MANUSCRIPTS OF THE THIRTEENTH CENTURY – T῾OROS AND STEP῾ANNOS VAHKAYC῾I

Among the manuscripts of the thirteenth century belonging to the Cilician period special attention should be focussed on four manuscripts which are the work of two compatriot artists from the same scriptorium, T῾oros and Step῾annos Vahkayc῾i.

Several circumstances favoured the increased artistic activity of the thirteenth century. The political situation was generally more relaxed and the country was economically more prosperous. The royal court and the prelates ordered scribes to copy manuscripts. Among these enlightened prelates whose career is particularly relevant to the discussion of these four manuscripts was Hovhannēs, the younger brother of Het῾um I, called Baldwin by his baptismal name, who was ordained bishop in 1259 for the district of Melevon, part of Barjrberd, in the mountainous region east of the Cilician gates. He was also appointed abbot of the nearby monastery of Gr̄ner. Hovhannēs' principal contribution to the artistic activities of his time was the creation and supervision of an important scriptorium at the monastery of Gr̄ner. From 1263 until his death in 1289 this scriptorium was one of the most active centres for the copying of manuscripts. A comprehensive list of those which have been preserved is provided by Prof. S. Der Nersessian in her discussion of MS FGA56.11 of the Freer Gallery of Art.[24]

The British Library's Add. MS 18549 is a manuscript of the New Testament copied on vellum 'in the year of the Armenians 729, in the metropolis of Sis, in the church of the Holy Spirit, which that same year was renovated with valuable stones polished by the artist Step῾annos Vahkayc῾i'. The scribe has also inserted his name in the short memorials on fols. 69b, 112a, 161a, 303b, and 308a. This manuscript has richly gilded illumination, is bright in colouring, and well drawn. The graceful headpieces, marginal arabesques, birds, decorative letters, were done in the thirteenth century by Step῾annos Vahkayc῾i. The five full-page portraits of the four evangelists, and of Peter and Paul, together with the pictures of saints in the margins of the Acts of the Apostles and the Catholic Epistles were added in Isfahān in 1618 by Mesrop of Khizan. The second half of the principal colophon states; 'I,Mesrop dpir Xizanc῾i again repaired and illuminated (*całkec῾i*) this manuscript with gold and *lapis lazuli* and all kinds of colours' (*see* PLATE VI).

The second manuscript in this group, although not a Gospel-book but an illuminated Breviary (Žamagirk῾) previously in the Hagob Kevorkian collection, is MS Or.13993, also copied by the scribe Step῾annos for King Lewon II/III of Cilician Armenia.[25] There is no precise indication of the place where

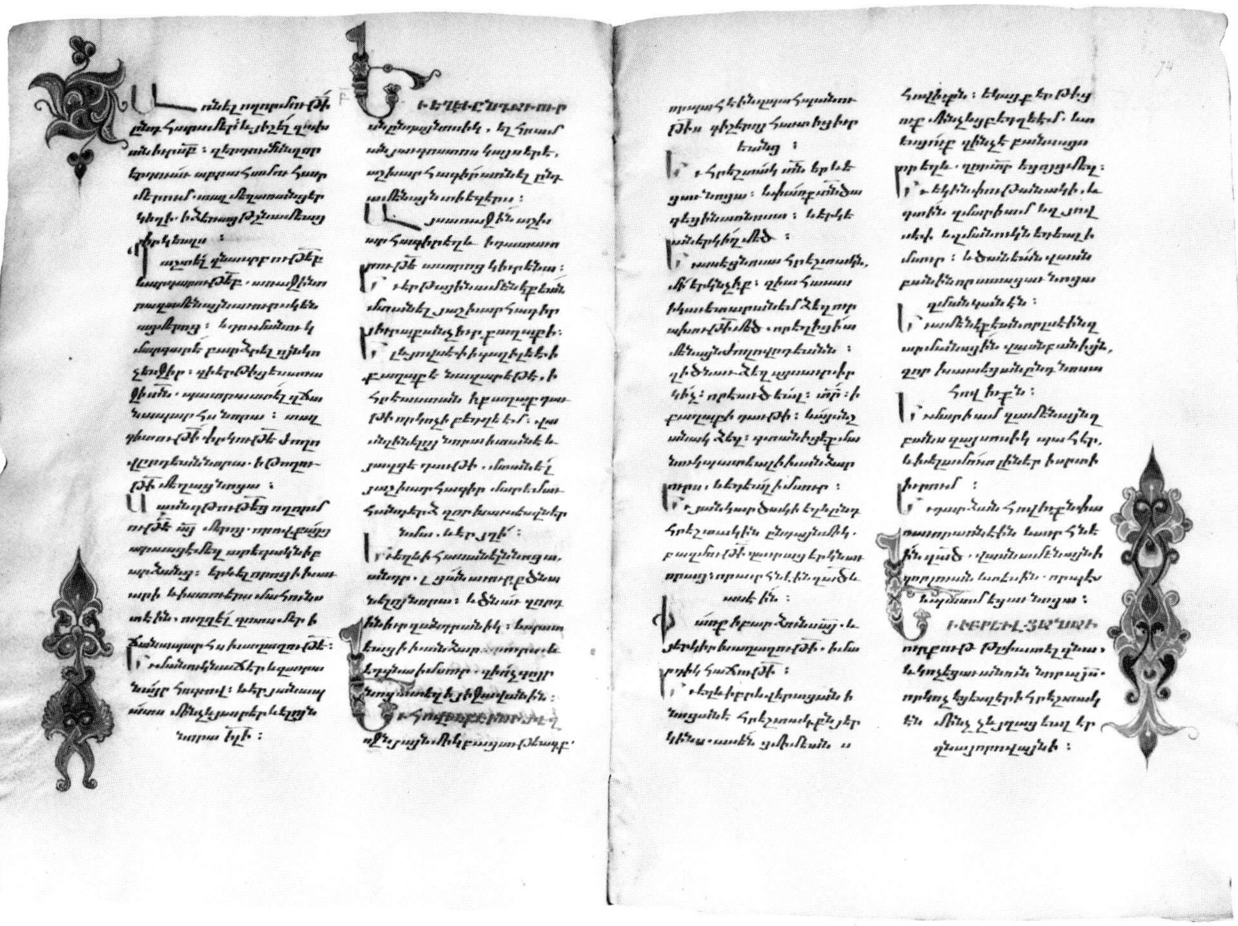

Fig. 7. *Four Gospels (Add. MS 18549).*
23 × 15·5 cm
fols. 73b–74a. Gospel of St Luke. Text written in elegant bolorgir, *in double columns* (1:72–80 *and* 2:1–21).

the manuscript was copied, or of its date.

The third of this group is MS Or.10960 and Add. MS 19730. Although these two manuscripts have separate numbers and were acquired at different times they are in my opinion a single manuscript which has been broken up into two parts.

Add. MS 19730 is a manuscript on thick glazed paper, much yellowed, written in large *bolorgir*, in double columns of twenty-nine lines each. The manuscript contains 187 folios (of which the last is blank), in eleven quires signed in the lower margins. The first quire, which contains folios 1–4, is signed as number 12, and the last number as 28.

The contents are as follows: Revelation (fol. 1), the Death of St John (fol. 18), Preface to the Paulines by Euthalius (fol. 22) followed by the Epistles from Romans to Philemon. Each of these Epistles except Romans is preceded by a list of contents. Fol. 128 begins with the Acts of the Apostles, followed by the Catholic Epistles. The manuscript has no principal colophon. There

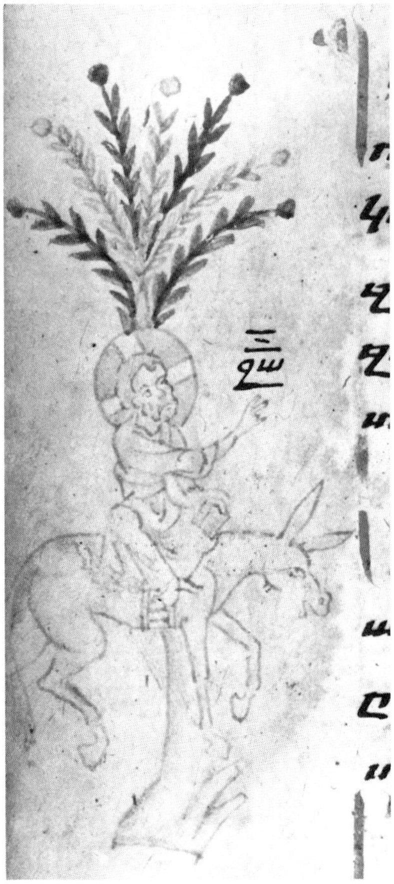

Fig. 8. *Four Gospels and the Book of Isaiah (MS Or.10960).*
24 × 17 cm.
fol. 27b. Jesus sitting on a donkey and a palm tree in the background: 'Tell the daughter of Zion, Behold, your king is coming to you humble, and mounted on an ass' (St Matthew 22:5–6).

are several short notices which give the name of the scribe as being Tʿoros Vahkaycʿi. The first of these and the most extensive is on fol. 18a, just before the text of 'The death of John the Apostle' which reads: 'O servants of God's word, for the love of Jesus Christ, remember the honourable priest Kostandin and all his kinsmen of the present and of the past, before the slain one, Jesus Christ; and myself, the worthless scribe Tʿoros and all the faithful, amen'. The name of the scribe is repeated in the memorial notices on fols. 45a, 120a, 166a, 183b, and 186b. This manuscript was purchased by the British Museum Library from Mr B. Barker in 1854. In 1928 the Library acquired MS Or.10960, the physical description of which is unmistakeably identical to Add. MS. 19730. It contains the Four Gospels (fols. 1–141b, John XI vv. 11–25 missing), followed by the Book of Isaiah (fols. 142–200b). There is no doubt that this manuscript is the first half of a New Testament manuscript, the second part of which is Add. MS 19730.

The principal colophon on fol. 201, an organic part of the manuscript, refers to personages whose dates may be regarded as an approximate *terminus post quem* for the original copying of the manuscript. According to this information the manuscript was presented by King Hetʿum II (1289–1307) to *marajaxt*, or marshal, Ōšin, Lord of Lambron. In the same colophon prayers are requested for 'king of Armenia Hetʿum and his God-fearing father and the king of Armenia Lewon (Leo II/III, 1270–89) and Keran his thrice blessed mother and queen of the Armenians. Also my father Baron Kostandin, Lord of Lambron and *tʿagadir* of the Armenians'. There have been two Kostandins with the title of *tʿagadir* (king-crowner). The first was Kostandin Lambronacʿi, who crowned King Hetʿum I, and was killed in 1250, The second was the husband of King Hetʿum's daughter Rita, Kostandin Sarvantikar, whose mother was Queen Keran, the daughter of Kostandin Lambronacʿi and Stepʿani. The son of this Kostandin, the marshal Ōšin is the owner of this manuscript, and the colophon 'this memorial of the Armenian era 744 (1295) was [written] by me Ōšin' testifies to that. The colophon continues and requests prayers for King Lewon II, his parents, King Hetʿum and Zabel (1219–1252); for his two sons, Kostandin and Hetʿum; his daughter, Tʿefanaw; his wife *tikin* Akacʿ; Fimi, the daughter of Hetum I and the wife of Julian, Lord of Sidon. In many ways this information repeats that contained in the colophon of MS M.740 in the Pierpont Morgan Library collection, written for Ōšin in 1274.[26] The name of the scribe, Tʿoros Vahkaycʿi, is repeated in several brief memorial notices (fols. 156b, 177b, 182a). In another comparatively extensive colophon he gives some biographical information about himself: 'unworthy scribe Tʿoros Vahkaycʿi and my departed relatives in Christ, my father Kostandin and my mother, and my father's brother (*hawr ełbayr*) Stepʿannos *kʿahanayn*'. The manuscript was written for the 'honourable priest Kiwrakos' (fols. 200b–201a).

The illustrations of this manuscript consist of five headpieces, marginal miniatures, ornate initials and attractive decoration. Of the headpieces the most attractive is the one over St Matthew's Gospel (PLATE V). Intricately interlaced leaves fill the headpiece, painted in green against the gold ground. Down the right-hand margin is an interlacing foliate motif crowned with an ornamental cross. The initial letter of St Matthew's Gospel, 'G', is an elegantly executed angel with wings and nimbus wearing a red tunic. The out-stretched hand holding a book forms the horizontal arm of the letter and in the other hand she holds a staff. The remaining text comprises five lines in double columns written in decorative uncials in gold outline, filled in blue and red. The headpieces of Mark (fol. 43) and Luke (fol. 70) are line drawings with their respective symbols forming the initial letters, while for the Gospel of John (fol. 114) all four symbols combine to form the letter 'I'. For the book of Isaiah, the first letter 'L' is composed of the figure of the prophet in a kneeling position. The marginal miniatures (three each in Matthew & Mark, eight in Luke, and four in John) are very interesting (Figs. 8, 9, 10, 11, 12).

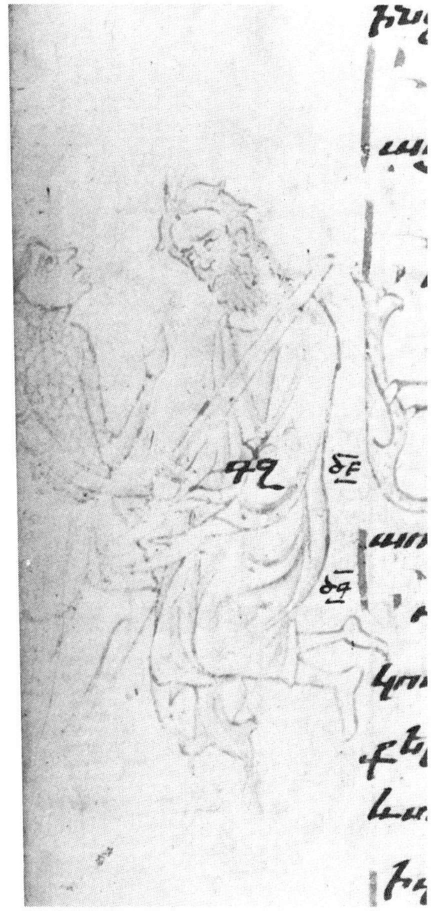

Fig. 9. *MS Or.10960.*
fol. 50b. John the Baptist kneeling in front of a soldier with raised sword (St Mark 6:27–28).

THE SCHOOL OF SIUNIKʿ—TʿOROS TARŌNACʿI

During the long rule of the Mongols in Greater Armenia, no important schools of illumination developed until the beginning of the fourteenth century. In the middle of the thirteenth century, when the Cilician schools flourished at Hṙomkla and Sis, a period of mutual rapport developed between the artists of Greater Armenia and that of Cilicia. The influence of Cilician painting spread to the different provinces of Greater Armenia. The provinces of Tarōn, Tayk, and Tourouberan had their scribes and artists among whom was a certain Yovhannēs, who in 1312 illuminated the Gospel MS 1949 of Jerusalem, with the portraits painted in Cilicia. The same is the case with MS 10 of the collection in the John Rylands Library. The cultural and artistic centre at this time in Greater Armenia was the monastery of Gladjor, situated in the Vayots djor, a district in the south-western part of Siunikʿ.[27] The foremost artist of this period was Tʿoros Tarōnacʿi or Mšecʿi,[28] who was born in Tarōn but lived first in Cilicia and then at the monastery of Gladjor where under the supervision of the famous scholar and abbot Esayi Nčʿecʿi he produced his best works. His artistic labours encompassed the years 1307–46, and eighteen manuscripts illustrated by him are known, one of which is Add. MS 15411, now in the British library.

This manuscript was copied for the priest Martiros 'in the famous and

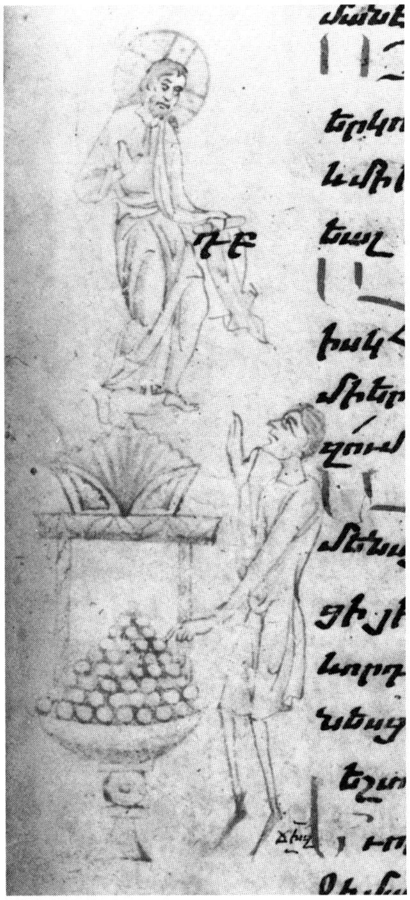

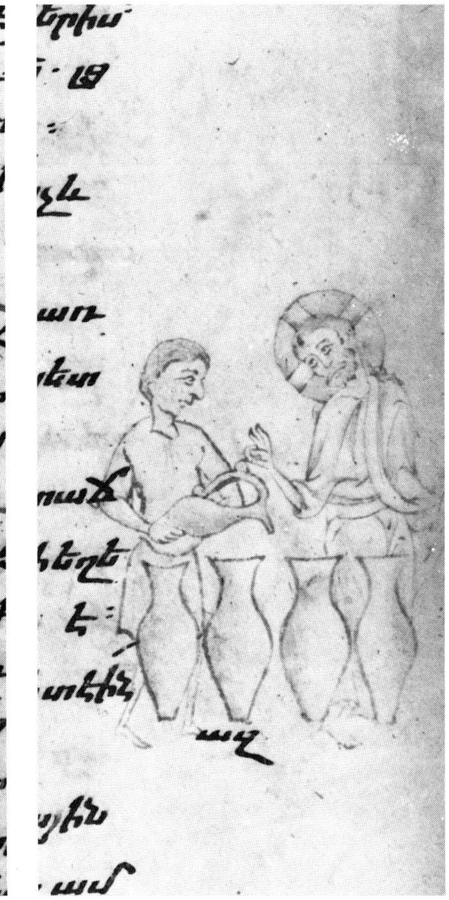

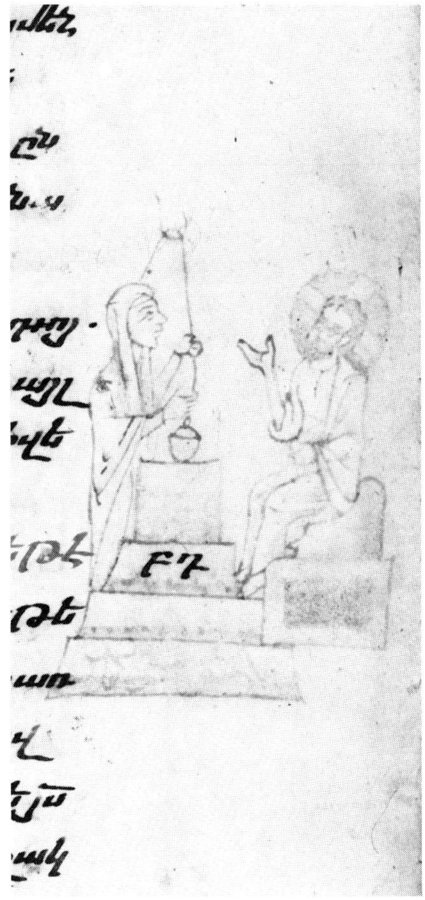

Fig. 10. (Left) *MS Or.10960. fol. 92b. Christ and one of the multitude who said to him 'Teacher, bid my brother divide the inheritance with me'* (St Luke 12:14–15).

Fig. 11. (Centre) *MS Or.10960. fol. 116a. Marriage at Cana, a servant pours water into a jug with Jesus looking on* (St John 2:7–8).

Fig. 12. (Right) *MS Or.10960. fol. 118a. Jesus sitting beside the well, with the woman of Samaria drawing water from the well* (St John 4:6–7).

holy cloister of the university of Gladjor' by the scribe Koriwn (not Kiwreł as deciphered by Conybeare and repeated by Yovsepʻeancʻ) in the '770th year of our era (AD 1321), in a bitter and untoward age, when the race of Archers exercised tyranny over the whole land of the Armenians and Iberians'. The manuscript, written on fine vellum in a neat *bolorgir*, was illustrated by Tʻoros Tarōnacʻi, who has included his signature in brief inscriptions beneath the portraits of St Matthew (fol. 9b) and St John (fol. 241b): 'Remember in the lord the painter of the holy pictures, Tʻoros'.

The manuscript is decorated as follows: the eight canon tables (fols. 1b–8a) are set between pilasters which support headpieces of blue scroll-work on a gold background, with pictures of pairs of partridges, cranes with fish in their mouths, cocks, winged lions drinking water out of a vase or a fountain. The outer margins are filled with palms and other trees on which peacocks are perched. The portraits of the evangelists precede their respective Gospels: St Matthew (fol. 9b), St Mark (fol. 91b) and St John (fol. 241b), with St Luke's missing. St Matthew and St Luke are shown seated in an architectural setting, an open book is placed on a lectern, the various implements on the desk, and each evangelist has a pen in one hand and a sheet of vellum in the other resting partly on their knees ready to write. In the case of St Matthew there is nothing written on the sheet of vellum or the open book which is placed on a lectern with a cock as a stand. In the case of St Mark's portrait the open book on the lectern has the words 'Jesus Christ' written in Greek uncials, while the first word of St Mark's Gospel, 'Skizb', is written in Armenian in large uncials. In the case of St John, T‘oros has adopted the composition generally used in Byzantine art after the eleventh century, that is, John standing in front of a rocky mountain and dictating to his disciple Prochoros, who is shown seated. The facial features are distinctive and well articulated.

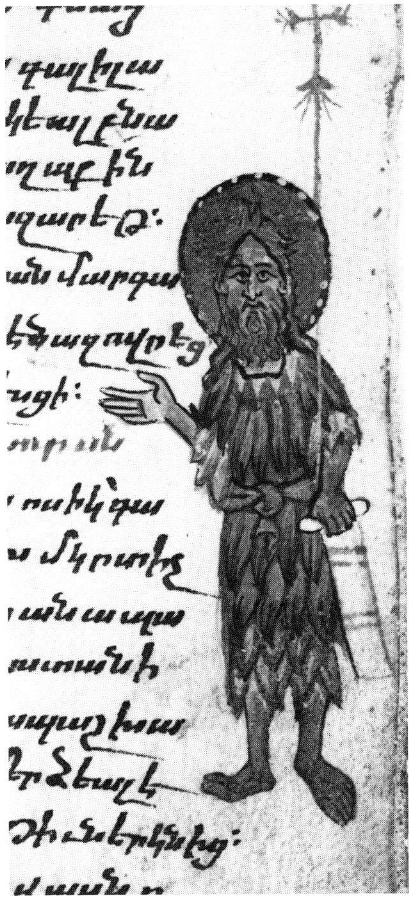

Fig. 13. *Four Gospels (Add. MS 15411).* *13·5 × 10·5cm.*
fol. 14a. John the Baptist, holding a cross and an open scroll (St Matthew 3:1–2).

The first page of each Gospel is marked by a headpiece richly decorated in a very distinctive style. The headpiece of St Mark is of especial interest (Fig. 14). In the middle of the headpiece the artist has represented the Virgin, enthroned, nursing the infant Jesus: she wears a red crown on her head with a halo and a long blue veil down over her shoulders covering the greater part of her red tunic. Two archangels dressed in imperial costumes, stand, one on each side, above the rectangle, and holding a chalice and a lance. The infant Jesus is seated on the Virgin's knee. She presents her breast to the Christ child, who has a scroll in his left hand and his right hand raised.

In an Armenian manuscript in the Case Memorial Library[29] of the Hartford Seminary Foundation, which is also the work of T‘oros Tarōnac‘i, completed in 1307, the image of the Virgin and Child is painted in the headpiece of the Gospel of St Matthew, while St Luke's headpiece has the Virgin holding Christ in her arms, His pressing-cheek against hers, designated as the Virgin of Tenderness. Prof. S. Der Nersessian[30] believes that the paintings of T‘oros Tarōnac‘i show the intrusion of western iconographic themes, which he probably saw in the manuscripts brought by the Latin missionaries who came to Armenia, or who resided for a time in Armenia on their way to the court of the Mongol Khans. For example, in the headpiece of St John's Gospel two sphinxes are set within, but, instead of using the eagle, T‘oros has introduced the symbols of the four evangelists. The eagle forms the loop of the first letter 'I', while the vertical bar is composed by the angel of St Matthew, the ox and the lion, standing one above the other, and an angel supporting with raised arms the enthroned Christ (PLATE VII). Occasionally the marginal ornamentations are replaced by pictures which are directly connected with the text. For instance small buildings are placed in the margins whenever the Temple of Jerusalem is mentioned. The figure of John the Baptist (Fig. 13) holds a cross and an open scroll and wears 'a garment of camel's hair' (fol. 14a). These are the two blind men from St Matthew IX:27 (fol. 30b), the two blind men of Jericho (fol. 61b), a shepherd boy (fol. 154b, Fig. 15) with his flock. To illustrate the marriage at Cana (*John II:5–6*), the painter has represented the bride

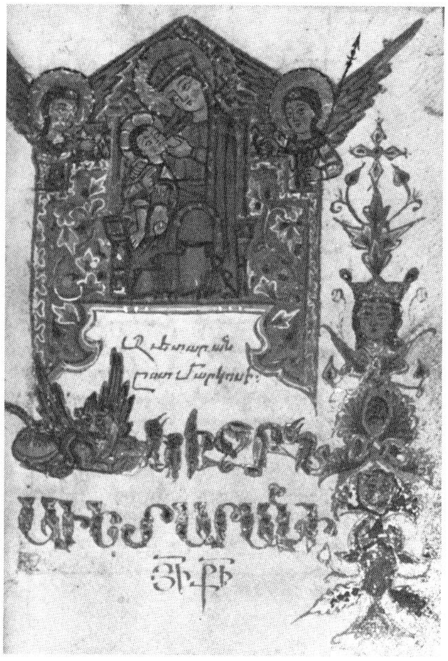

Fig. 14. *Add. MS 15411. fol. 92a. Headpiece of St Mark's Gospel.*

Fig. 15. *Add. MS 15411. fol. 154b. A shepherd boy and two sheep* (St Luke 2:8).

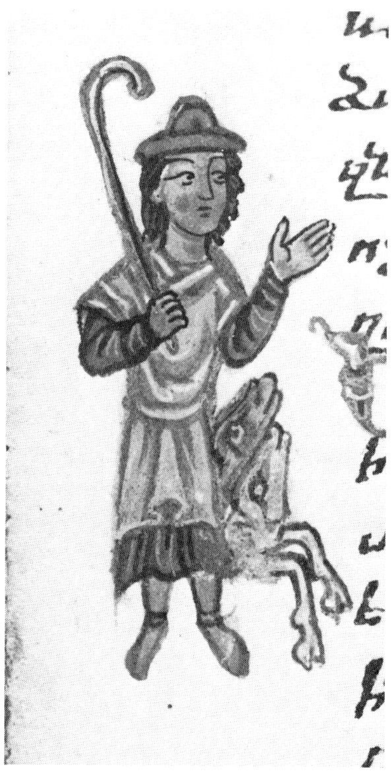

and the bridegroom, wearing crowns decorated with a cross and seated under a stylised arbour (fol. 246a) with seven jars placed in a row below (PLATE VIII); for the Entry into Jerusalem (*John XII:12–14*) a boy is represented holding a palm leaf (fol. 282b, Fig. 16), and to illustrate the verse 'So they took Jesus, and he went out, bearing his own Cross' a young Jesus is depicted holding aloft in one hand a cross and an open scroll in the other (fol. 302b). This great variety of ornamental motifs and pictures demonstrate the imagination and inventiveness of Tʿoros Tarōnacʿi.

THE ARTIST AWAG *Całkoł*

Tʿoros Tarōnacʿi is not the only artist of Siunikʿ. Several other artists, such as Sargis, Momik, Kirakos of Tabriz, Mxitʿar of Ani, Tʿoros *sarkawag*[31] (i.e. the deacon) are a few of the artists of Greater Armenia. Among these the work of Awag has a special place and is admirably represented by MS Or.5304. According to information contained in colophons the painter Awag was by birth from Mušałbiwr,[32] a locality in the eastern section of Vayots Djor, in the province of Siunikʿ, and he attended the university of Gladjor as a pupil of Esayi Nčʿecʿi. He worked not only in Siunikʿ but also in Cilicia, the Crimea, and between the years 1329 and 1358 at Sultʿaniya (Atrpatakan and Pʿaytakaran) in western Iran. For this reason L. A. Durnova calls Awag 'the wandering artist'. R. Drambian and G. Yovsepʿeancʿ, bearing in mind the fact that Awag was a pupil of Esayi Nčʿecʿi, link him with the Gladjor school. A. N. Avetisyan has listed seven manuscripts belonging to Awag painted between 1329 and 1358.[33] Of these five are in Erevan, one in the Berlin Royal Library and one is a Bible in Venice. To this must be added British Library MS Or.5304, a manuscript of the New Testament, without date. To this manuscript, F. C. Conybeare assigned the years 1400–1500. The name of the scribe is written at the end of the Letter of Eusebius– 'I beseech you to remember Awag the painter and scribe'; this inscription, which allows us to date the manuscript more accurately, had escaped the attention of Conybeare.[34]

The Cilician influence in Awag's miniatures is even stronger than in those of Tʿoros Tarōnacʿi, for they were inspired by the works of Tʿoros Roslin. Like the latter he also illustrates the story of the Gospel in great detail, with narrative miniatures inserted into the text and in the margins. MS Or.5304 contains over fifty miniatures, each of the Gospels with its own cycle of miniatures illustrating vividly and dramatically in rapid sequence the story told in the text (see Appendix B, Fig. 17 and PLATE IX–X).

Political events interrupted the activities of the monasteries of Siunikʿ and neighbouring regions. Relations with the Mongols deteriorated when the latter adopted the Muslim religion. The rivalries betweeen the leaders of different Mongol tribes, and the revolts of local rulers caused constant struggles. Armenia was often a battlefield. In 1021 Senekerim, the last monarch of the Vaspurakan kingdom, hard pressed by the Seljuks, ceded his kingdom to Basil II, receiving in exchange the city of Sebastia in Cappadocia.[35] In 1045 the last king of Ani Gagik was lured to Constantinople with false promises and in his absence Ani, the capital of the Bagradit kingdom, was annexed to the Empire.

Economic conditions began to improve slowly when the Mongols chose the southern caravan route for their trade in the second half of the thirteenth century. This route passed near Arčēš on the north bank of Lake Van. One by one scriptoria were set up, first at Arčēš, then at Ałtʿamar and at the monasteries on the islands of Lake Van and in the towns in the vicinity.

Manuscripts copied here, on paper rather than parchment, contrast with the lavish volumes produced in other parts of Armenia and in Cilicia. MS Or.2679 of the British Library collection is a manuscript dated 1281 which was copied in the canton of Arčēš at the monastery of Yaspisenkal, during the prelacy of Father Abraham. The second colophon (fol. 291) records how 'in this bitter and *tartaros* age, in the year of the Armenians 795 [AD 1346], the entire country was ruined and desolated everywhere by the blood drinking race of Archers (Tartars)' this Gospel fell into the hands of priest Stepʿanos who had it 'with the earnings of his honest labour and toil illuminated afresh and bound'.

The initial illumination of this manuscript was very simple. It consisted of the arcades painted for the Letter of Eusebius, and small oblong headpieces accompanied by long page-length initial letters marking the beginning of each Gospel (fols. 6, 82, 132, 223). The rest of the decoration was added in the fourteenth or fifteenth century. This includes the headpiece on fol. 5b with a central arcade, which, instead of containing text, has a crude picture of the evangelist St Matthew; a figure of the Virgin Mary (fol. 81b, see Figs. 18 and 19); a similar figure on fol. 131b, probably that of St Luke whose Gospel begins on fol. 132a; and fol. 222a is a set headpiece under which are the figures of St John and Prochoros in the same style as the frontispiece of St Matthew. All the marginal arabesques, figures, shrines, and branches that mark the forty-two lessons of each Gospel are also of later origin. The manuscript was given to the church of Holy Astuacacin in Yuṙhay (i.e. Edessa) in 1553 by 'David who bought the manuscript and four silver plaques and a cross which they

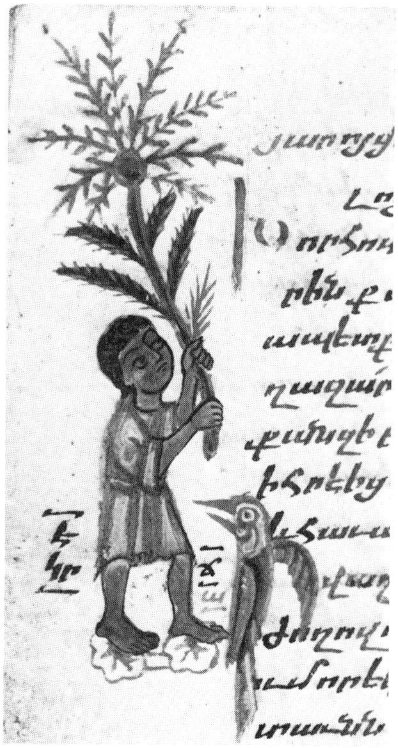

Fig. 16. *Add. MS 15411.*
fol. 282b. Entry into Jerusalem. A boy holding a palm branch (St John 12:12–14).

Fig. 17. *Four Gospels (MS Or.5304).*
23·5 × 15·5 cm.
fol. 27a. The healing of the paralytic. Two men on the roof letting down the pallet on which the paralytic lies; Christ standing while three onlookers squat on the right (St Mark 2:1–5).

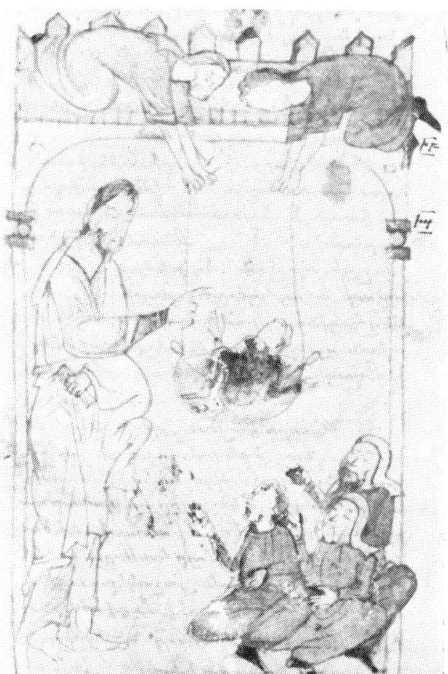

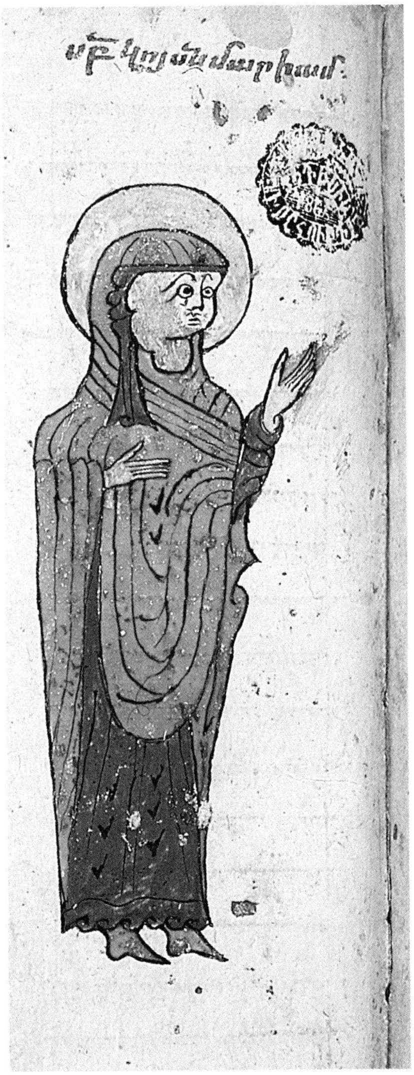

Fig. 18. *Four Gospels (MS Or.2679). 23 × 16 cm.*
fol. 81b. An Egyptian-like figure, in red and green, preceding the Gospel of St Mark. Above her head the inscription reads 'Holy Virgin Mary'.

nailed on' (now missing). On fol. 5b, 81b, and IIIa there is an imprint of an Armenian stamp, with the legend 'Tʿałakan xorhurd Yedesia 1866'. This stamp is found also on MSS Or.2669, 2680, 2681, and 2678, which were all acquired by the library in 1883, from the Revd. Sukias Baronian.

The second manuscript that conforms to the Vaspurakan type is MS Or.2680 with its extremely interesting miniatures. The manuscript in question was copied in the year 1317 by the scribe Astuacatur, in *bolorgir*, as was customary at that time. The artistic work is crude, though still quite lively and effective, closely related to the prototypes Erevan 2744 (AD 1305) and 4806 (AD 1306).

Among the distinctive features of Vaspurakan book illustration is the position of the historiated miniatures. The miniatures depicting the major episodes of the life of Christ, grouped in a multiple frontispiece, are placed at the beginning, preceding the canon tables. Fols. 2b–5b carry the eleven scenes forming the cycle illustrating major events in the life of Christ, mounted in the vertical fashion, so that the picture is seen sideways, with the spine of the book running along the feet of the figures. Since the feet in both illustrations fall to the same edge of the folio, when the page is turned, rotating the folio around the spine of the book, the other side comes out upside down. Another distinctive feature is the compositional device, the presentation of two scenes on the same page without break. The Gospel cycle in this manuscript consists of the Nativity & the Adoration of the Magi, Presentation in the Temple & the Baptism of Christ, the Transfiguration & the Raising of Lazarus, Christ's entry into Jerusalem, the Last Supper & Christ washing the disciples' feet, the Betrayal, the Crucifixion and the Entombment.

There is evidence that the artist of MS Or.2680 at times misread the illustrations he was copying, and produced a muddled result. In the Transfiguration scene (fol. 3b) the figure representing Moses is depicted standing in a blue winding sheet like the figure of Lazarus on the right hand of the page; in the Crucifixion (fol. 5b) two crosses are shown instead of three, and Mary is represented with halo. The fact that in some cases where the Gospel pictures are paired, the right hand picture precedes the left, and that also in the case of the Entry into Jerusalem, Christ moves from right to left, suggests a possible Syriac antecedent for some of the iconography, where the flow of the writing and hence the temporal progress of the narrative is from right to left. The paintings of this manuscript are characterised by simplicity in presentation, the figures are drawn frontally with wide and expressive eyes, the emphasis being on outline with background detail completely absent (PLATES XI–XII).[36]

Another manuscript belonging to the more conservative trend is MS Or.2707 copied by the scribe Karapet in 1541 'in the land of Bžunikʿ, now called Xlatᶜ (Ahlat)' situated north of Lake Van. The illustration of the manuscript 'elegantly executed with lavish use of gold' begins with the canon tables, including the text of Stepᶜannos Bishop of Siunikᶜ, symbolic interpretation of the decorations of the canons, followed by the seventeen full-page miniatures illustrating the life of Jesus (see Appendix C). The cycle begins with the Vision of Ezekiel and the Tree of Jesse (PLATE XIII). Early commentators on the scriptures maintained that the Gospel events were the fulfilment of Old Testament prophecy. 'As Moses lifted up the serpent in the wilderness, even so must the Son of Man be lifted up'; thus, according to St John's Gospel, did Christ foretell his Crucifixion in terms of the occasion when Moses saved the people of Israel by the raising of the brazen serpent. By means of similar juxtaposition 'as Jonah was three days and three nights in the belly of the whale, so shall the son of Man be three days and three nights in the hearth of the earth'. In the Old Testament the New lies hidden; in the New Testament the Old becomes clear. 'What Moses veils, the teaching of Christ unveils'.

The Vision of Ezekiel represented the Second Coming of Christ. Christ is depicted enthroned in the innermost part of three concentric circles which represent 'the wheel within the wheel'; the tetramorphs are drawn in the diagonal axes, their bodies cut by the second circle and their wings projecting beyond the outer circle. Ezekiel lies in the foreground, by the banks of the river Qobar, and the open scroll is held by a hand emerging from under the outermost circle (*Ezekiel 2.9–3.3*). The second Old Testament theme is the Tree of Jesse, which is of course an illustration of one of the most famous prophecies of the coming of Christ: 'And there shall come forth a rod out of the stem of Jesse, and a branch shall grow out of his roots'. In the miniature (PLATE XIV) the tree, sprouting from Jesse's side, divides at the top into two branches above which are the figures of the Virgin and Child; six ancestors stand one above the other next to the trunk of the tree, while others are represented under small arches or inside small medallions which cover the entire field.

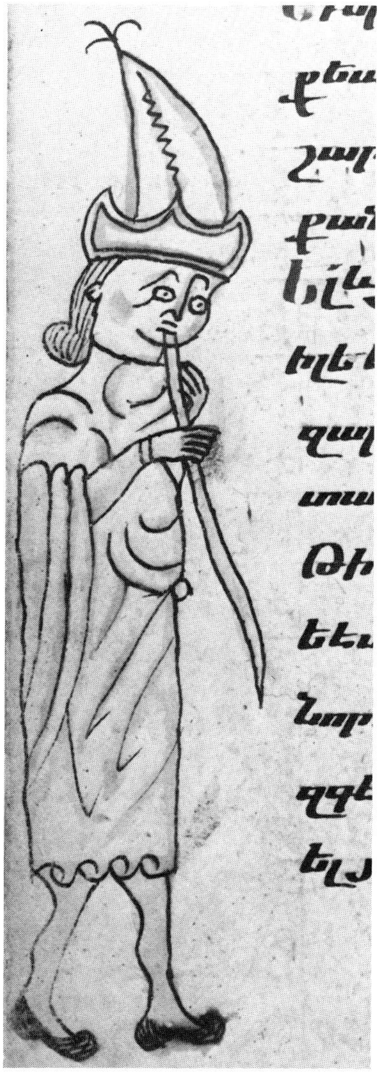

Fig. 19. *MS. Or.2679 fol. 137b. A shepherd boy playing the flute* (St Luke 2:8–9).

THE SCHOOL OF KHIZAN

The second branch of the Van school, called the 'Khizan school' comprising manuscripts copied in Khizan (Hizan), south of Lake Van, and in the canton of Mokᶜ(Mukus), is represented in the British Library collection by several manuscripts, the most important being MS Or.82 and MS Or.5737. The first is illustrated by Martiros of Khizan, 'the recognised master of the Khizan school in the late sixteenth and early seventeenth centuries'. The manuscript is richly illuminated with canon tables, headpieces and full-page portraits of each of

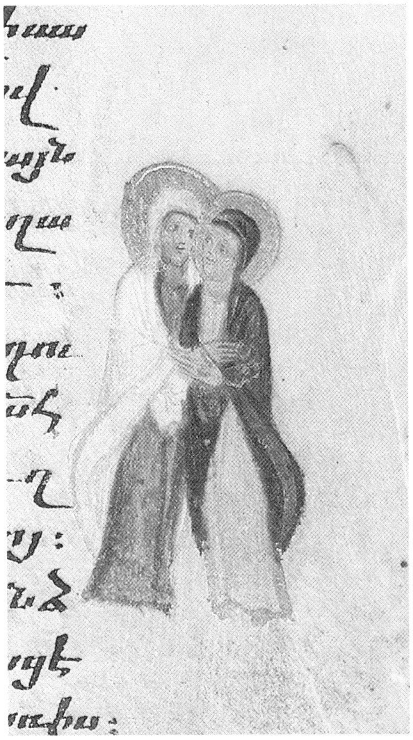

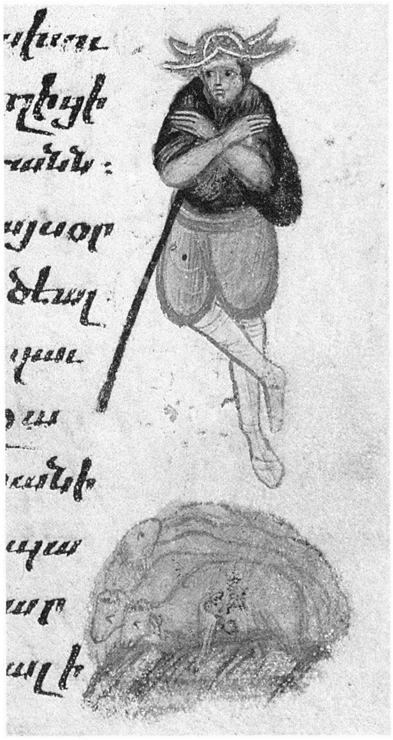

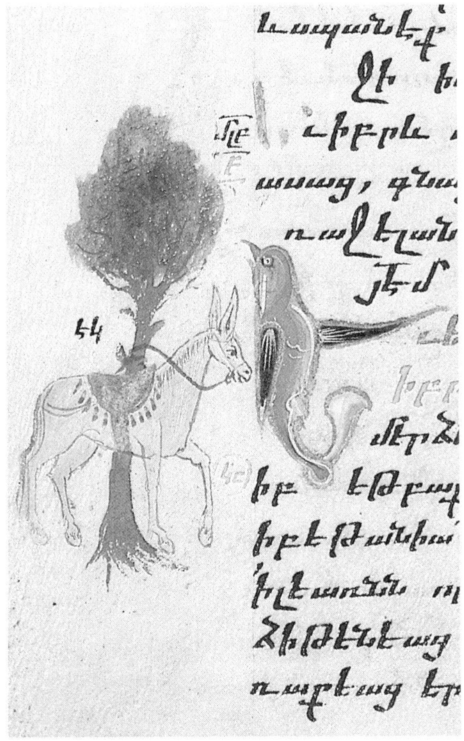

Fig. 20. (Left) *Four Gospels (MS Or.82).* *15·5 × 10·5 cm.* *fol. 140a. Mary and Elizabeth* (St Luke 1:39–40).

Fig. 21. (Centre) *MS Or.82.* *fol. 143a. Shepherd, and sheep grazing* (St Luke 2:8–9).

Fig. 22. (Right) *MS Or.82.* *fol. 206b. A colt tied to a tree* (St Luke 19:28–29).

the evangelists. The headpiece of St Matthew, most delicately executed, is decorated with golden pomegranates with leaves drawn in the free spaces on a blue background. A good miniature of the Virgin and Child occupies the centre of the rectangle. The large initial letter of the text is formed by the figure of a saint in red and blue tunic holding up a book, while the rest of the line is completed in festooned letters of great beauty. Among the marginal miniatures the most interesting are the depiction of the shepherd boy (fol. 143a, Fig. 21), the Entry into Jerusalem (fol. 206b, Fig. 22), and the Annunciation (fol. 140a, Fig. 20). The workmanship of these is excellent (see Appendix B).

THE SCHOOLS OF THE DIASPORA: THE SCHOOL OF NEW JULFA

The activities of the Khizan scriptoria diminished after the first quarter of the seventeenth century, though the scribes continued to work in the neighbouring province of Mokʿ. The wars between the Turks and the Persians, and the mass deportations carried out by Shah 'Abbas in 1604–05, caused havoc among the population. The Armenians deported by Shah 'Abbas were settled in the suburbs of Isfahān, the new capital of Persia.

British Library MS Or. 5737, copied in Isfahān, and Bodleian Library MS Arm.d.13 copied in 1609 by Mesrop, who was among the 2000 families deported by Shah 'Abbas, recalls the event in the colophon thus: 'Mourning fell upon Armenia, for he destroyed and made desolate all houses and habi-

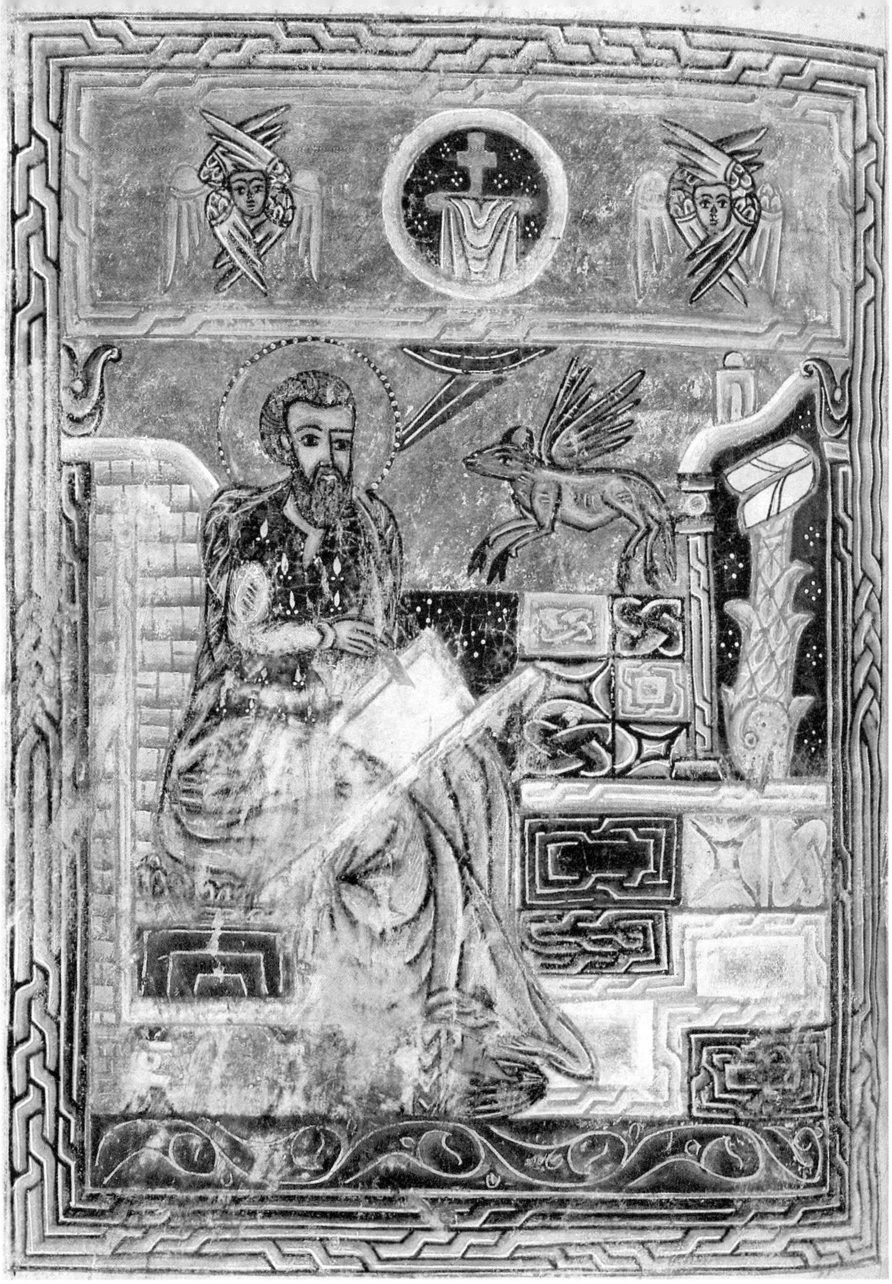

Fig. 23. *Four Gospels (MS Or.5737).*
23·5 × 18 cm.
fol. 156b. Portrait of St Luke

tations, so that men fled and hid themselves in fortresses and clefts of rocks. Some he found and slew, others he led captive and sent to that city of Šoš or Aspahan . . . And he settled us on the south side of the river Zander . . . where we built houses and habitations and churches for prayers'.

The manuscript begins with a set of seventeen full-page miniatures followed by the Letter of Eusebius, the canon tables, the portraits and headpieces for each of the four Gospels. The decoration is remarkably executed in bright colours of green, red, yellow, and blue set on a gold background, and each picture is framed in a border of interlacing lines and scrollwork. The human figures are crudely drawn and it is obvious that while Mesrop was a prolific artist as far as ornamentation was concerned, he had 'little ability in drawing human figures'.

In the Last Judgement (PLATE XVI), the Ancient of Days is seated inside a rectangular frame, holding a book in one hand and pronouncing a blessing with the other, enthroned on the four apocalyptic beasts, each of which holds a book. The Virgin and John the Baptist stand one at each side with open arms in an attitude of supplication. The scales hang from the lower band of the frame; two demons try to pull down the right-hand tray with a hook; and the left-hand tray rests on the back of another demon. An angel on the left pierces both demons with his lance. The inscription above reads: 'The Last Judgement'. In the Presentation in the Temple (PLATE XV) the Virgin and Joseph (with no representation of doves) Simeon with the boy Christ in his arms, and prophetes's Anna, holding a scroll, stand beside a table placed under two conical shaped domes.

In the portraits the evangelists are seated before a desk writing with their respective symbols placed above the lecterns. Luke (Fig. 23) is also seated, writing, before a desk, with a lectern resting on a fish and next to it a winged ox on a gold background. In the upper half of the miniature, separated by a narrow band, is drawn in the centre an altar with veil and cross framed within circles, and at the sides two tetramorphs.

An interesting element in the illustration of this manuscript is the inclusion of incipits from the text of the symbolic explanation of the ten canon tables in the lower margins of each canon. In Armenian literature we know the names of three authors who composed commentaries on the meaning of the ten canon tables. The first, *Meknutʿ iwn xoranacʿ Awetaranin* by Stepʿannos Bishop of Siunikʿ (688–735) is found in several manuscripts up till the end of the thirteenth century. In the twelfth century Nersēs Šnorhali (1166–1173) in the introduction to his commentary on the Gospel of St Matthew added a new explanation called *Meknutʿiwn saks tasn xoranacʿ*, which was published in Constantinople in 1825.[37] In this commentary Nersēs suggests that the ten canon tables, with their detailed decorations and colour scheme, should reflect the Church and its typological relations with the Old Testament. He then gives the exact meaning of each canon as follows: Canon I, the Trinity; II & III, angels; IV, the image of the Garden; V, Noah's ark; VI, altar of Abraham; VII, Aaron and Moses, VIII, altar with the tables of the law; IX, a Temple; X, a Church. Each one of these canons is then considered separately and symbolic explanations are given for the colours and for the component elements of the decorations. Nersēs emphasises that four colours are to be used – red, green, black, and blue – and purple separately from the other four: four types of trees – palm, olive, pomegranate, and lily; and six types of birds – peacock, dove, partridge, cock, albatross and hen.[38]

After Nersēs Šnorhali the author Grigor Tatʿewacʿi (1346–1409) in his Commentary on the Gospel of St Matthew, when commenting on the Eusebian

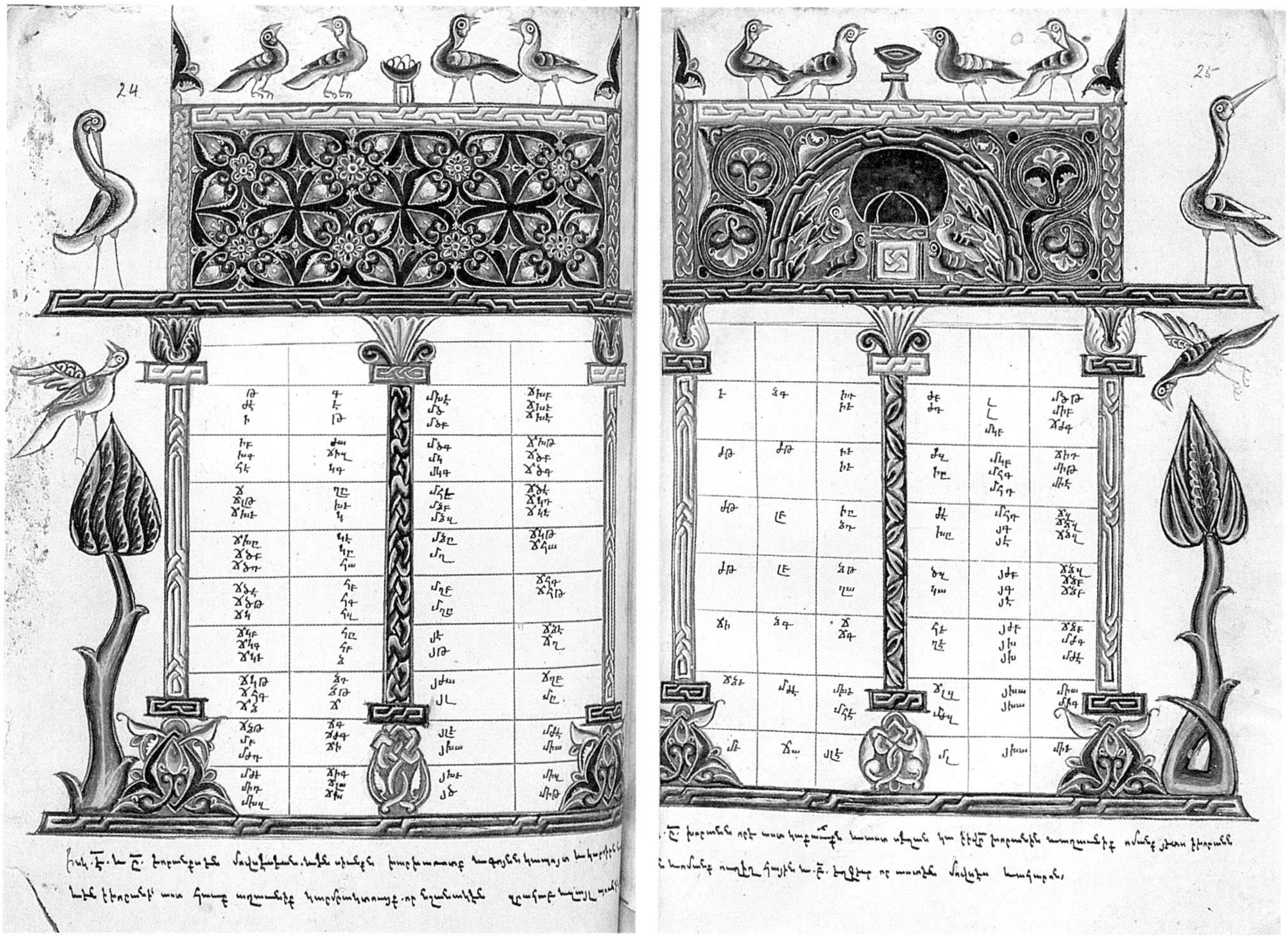

Fig. 24. *MS Or.5737*
fols. 24b–25a. The Canon Tables, no. vii–viii.

concordance tables, concludes the section with *Vasn tas xoranacʿn ew zanazan gunocʿ* (On the ten canon tables and the various colours) which is an abridgment of Nersēs's work. It is this abbreviated version that occurs below the margins of some manuscripts including MS Or.2707[39] and MS Or.5737. In this manuscript illustrated by Mesrop of Khizan, the Trinity replaces the portrait of Eusebius, in conformity with the brief notice written in the lower margin, while the portraits of Eusebius and Carpianus adorn the second rectangle. Over the rectangle of the eight canon (Fig. 24) there is an altar with horns, and birds flying round it. The explanation written under this canon reads: 'the altar and the doves; some of them look back to the altar; some look ahead. The two horns represent Moses and Aaron'.

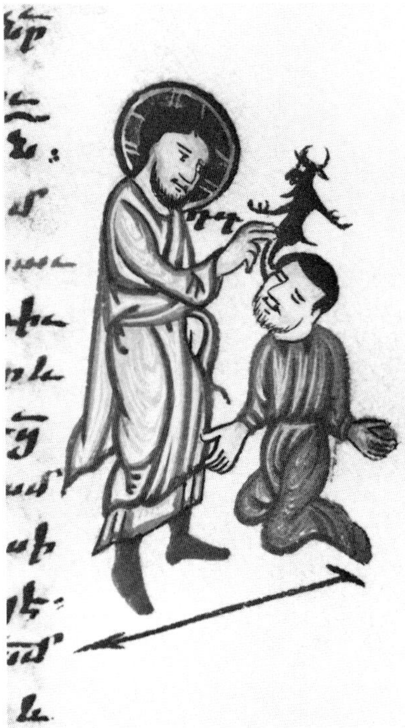

Fig. 25. *Four Gospels (MS Or.14161).* *8 × 5 cm.*
fol. 56a. Jesus healing the blind and dumb demoniac (St Matthew 12:22).

In 1618 Mesrop 'repaired afresh' and 'illuminated with gold and *lapis lazuli* and all sorts of colours in unison' Add. MS 18549, a manuscript written at Sis in 1280 (*see* PLATE VI). Similarly Add. MS 15,411 of 1321 was also 'adorned with gold and jewels in the year 1520 at Isfahān'. This is evidence that the wealthy Armenian merchants of New Julfa acquired fine manuscripts written in Cilicia and Greater Armenia and had them restored and repaired by local artists. The artists of New Julfa copied the ornamental designs of the Cilician manuscripts with the utmost fidelity: only the imitation of the figure style of the Cilician artists, and their attempt to give convincing form, occasionally result in figures with bulging hips and swollen knees.

THE SCHOOLS OF CONSTANTINOPLE AND CRIMEA

In addition to New Julfa there were other Armenian centres in Constantinople and the Crimea where there was a general revival of manuscript painting in the seventeenth century. The Armenian community of Constantinople increased greatly after the establishment of the Armenian Patriarchate in 1461, when regular scriptoria were founded. Manuscripts originating in Constantinople have the same characteristics as those copied in New Julfa. The old Armenian tradition of grouping the important scenes at the beginning of the Gospel still continued, though the cycle had been enlarged by the addition of several miniatures, particularly on the theme of the Holy Week (Washing of the Feet, the Last Supper, the Betrayal, the Road to Calvary) and scenes connected with the Second Coming (Christ in Glory, the Last Judgement).

Among these manuscripts displaying western influences are MSS Or. 13895(1658), Or.5449(1683), Or.14161(1695), and Or.13808. MS Or.5449, almost certainly copied in New Julfa, has multiple frontispieces consisting of sixteen full-page miniatures (see Appendix B and C) which end with two pictures representing the Second Coming of Christ or Christ in Glory (fol. 15b, PLATE XVII) and the Last Judgement (fol. 16a). The first composition illustrates the text of St Matthew's Gospel: 'And then shall appear the sign of the Son of man in heaven . . . and they shall see the Son of man coming in the clouds of heaven with power and great glory. And he shall send his angels with a great sound of a trumpet, and they shall gather together his elect from the four winds, from one end of heaven to the other' (*XXIV:30–31*). A large ornate cross in gold represents the 'sign of the Son of Man' raised on a seven-stepped pedestal. In each angle made by the cross there is an angel playing a trumpet and below, to the left and right, are two supplicants, the donors of the manuscript, with their names 'Baron Aławelin, and his partner in life Xanpʿar Xačʿik' inscribed in white above their heads. The same identical miniature occurs in Add, MS 7940 (fol. 15b) and also in an earlier manuscript, MS Or.2707 (fol. 22).

The Last Judgement scene usually occupies the opposite page. Christ is shown enthroned; at his sides are the Virgin and John the Baptist standing in an attitude of prayer; behind them stand the apostles. Below, against the blue background, Adam and Eve kneel at the sides of an empty throne and an angel holds the scales. The river of fire issues from Christ's throne and flows into the open jaws of a dragon in the lower right corner. A group of saints approaches a walled enclosure inside which is seated Abraham, holding a large cloth. A red seraph is guarding the gate (fol. 16).

This same model is also found in MS Or.14161, a manuscript with a very interesting provenance. The manuscript is dated 1695 and was copied by the scribe Xačʿatur *dpir* at the church of St George called *Sulu Manastir* in Constantinople. The artist is named in the colophon as the 'worthless scribe and artist' (*gcoł ew nkaroł*) Gabriēl, who names his father as being Markos *patkerahan* (the portraitist) and his newly-born son as Minas. The same name and epithets occur in Vienna, Mkhitharist MS 319 painted at the same place in 1694.[40] A folded nineteenth-century notice in French glued between the front cover and fly-leaf contains a quotation from Jean Duchesne's *Voyage d'un iconophile* which cites William III, King of England, Scotland and Ireland, 1688–1702, as the owner of the manuscript. In 1849 the manuscript was in the possession of M. Brisard of Ghent as MS 4 of his collection, and later according to a description by Henry Gough dated June 1873 the manuscript passed into the library of the Marquess of Bute as MS 84(G.14).[41] It has recently been acquired by the British Library. This manuscript has sixteen full-page miniatures and over fifty marginal scenes (see Appendix B and C).

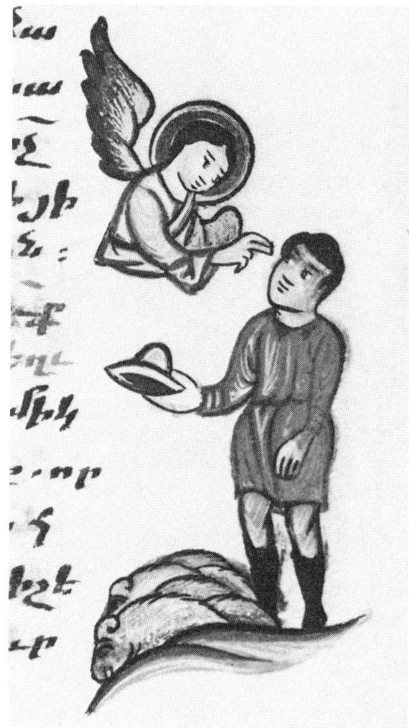

Fig. 26. *MS Or.14161. fol. 164a. A shepherd boy with hat in hand, looking up to an angel above his head, below, sheep grazing* (St Luke 2:8–9).

Western iconographic influences are discernible in various details. The angel of the Annuciation carries a bunch of lilies (fol. 1b); in the Crucifixion (fol. 12a) Christ is fixed to the cross with three nails; Mary touches the thigh of Christ; in the Resurrection picture (instead of the Harrowing of Hell) Christ is shown triumphantly rising from the tomb holding a bannered cross, while soldiers are searching the empty tomb with its lid of marble. The artist's style is meticulous, and has a sense of the dramatic. In all the small scenes connected with the act of healing, in which the exorcism of demons is involved, the artist has depicted the demon as a tiny black beast (fols. 56a, 171b, 196b, etc., Fig. 25). Quite dramatic and unique is the depiction of Judas committing suicide (PLATE XVIII). He is shown hanging from a tree standing on the back of a demon, with the pieces of silver (painted in gold) strewn beneath the feet of the demon (fol. 98a). The most interesting among the marginal miniatures is

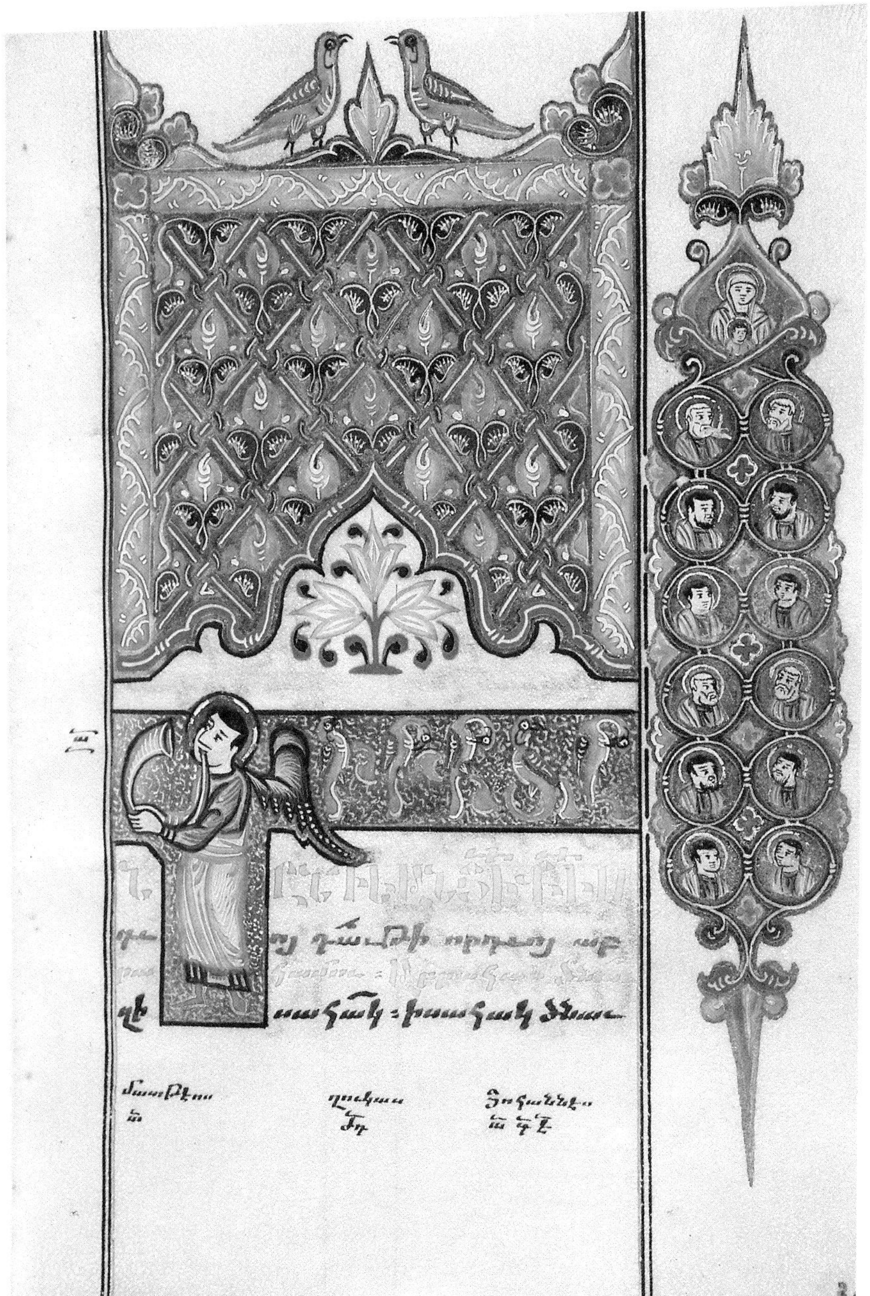

Fig. 27. *MS Or.14161.*
fol. 31a. Headpiece of St Matthew's Gospel, with initial letter 'G' formed of the Evangelist's symbol, and an accompanying full length arabesque in the margin with twelve busts of the ancestors of Christ and Mary with the Child.

the portrait of St John the Baptist, winged like an angel, and holding a scroll with the inscription: 'a voice crying in the wilderness' (fol. 34b). This iconographic type is based on the prophecy of Malachi (*III:1*) repeated by St Matthew (*XI:10*): 'Behold, I send my messenger and he shall prepare the way before me'. In the writings of the church fathers John is referred to as 'an angel incarnate' who, at the time of the Baptism, was assisted by angels, for 'he performed the service in an angelic way though still within human life'. The figure of St John in the fourth Gospel (fol. 243b) belongs to another mode. Here he is depicted without the wings or scroll; instead he has in his hand a small disc on which is drawn the image of the lamb ('Amnes'), a reference to St John's proclamation 'Behold, the lamb of God, who takes away the sins of the world' (*I:29*). In the portraits of the evangelists the respective symbols are represented crouching at the feet of the evangelists, following the type well-known from European engravings.

Among the seventeenth-century Gospel-books in the British Library pride of place is reserved for MS Or.13895. The manuscript was written and illuminated by the scribe Nikołayos, calling himself *całkarar* or *melanawor*, in 1658,[42] in Kaffa (Crimea). He was the principal representative of the Crimean school, and active from the 1640s up to his death in 1693. He worked mainly in the scriptorium attached to the church of St Sargis at Theodosia (Kaffa) and in Surxatʿ. Between the years 1647 and 1693 he copied and illuminated over thirty-four manuscripts, thirty of which are now kept in the collection at Erevan. According to Korxmazyan, after the downfall of the Cilician kingdom in 1375 and before that the fall of the Bagradit monarchy in 1045 large numbers of Armenians settled in the Crimea, taking with them a rich collection of Armenian manuscripts. Here was inspiration for Nikołayos, who modelled his illuminations on Cilician manuscripts of the thirteenth century.

The Gospel cycle at the beginning of MS Or.13895 comprises the principal scenes of Christ's life from the Annunciation to the Pentecost and two miniatures depicting the Second Coming. The Resurrection is illustrated by means of repitition of the Harrowing of Hell placed immediately after the miniature of the Crucifixion, a sequence suggesting that Christ descended into Hell as soon as He had died on the Cross. The two miniatures selected here to represent this manuscript depict the Ascension (PLATE XIX(a)) and the Pentecost (PLATE XIX(b)).[43] Of these two miniatures, that of the Pentecost merits special attention. The main feature in the iconography of the Armenian Pentecost miniature is a zoomorphic figure with human body but animal head which makes its appearance in the last quarter of the thirteenth century. The figure is found among the 'pious men of all nations' who were sojourning in Jerusalem, traditionally placed under the arc formed below the feet of the twelve Apostles seated in a semi-circle. The semi-naked figure, which appears to be a demon,

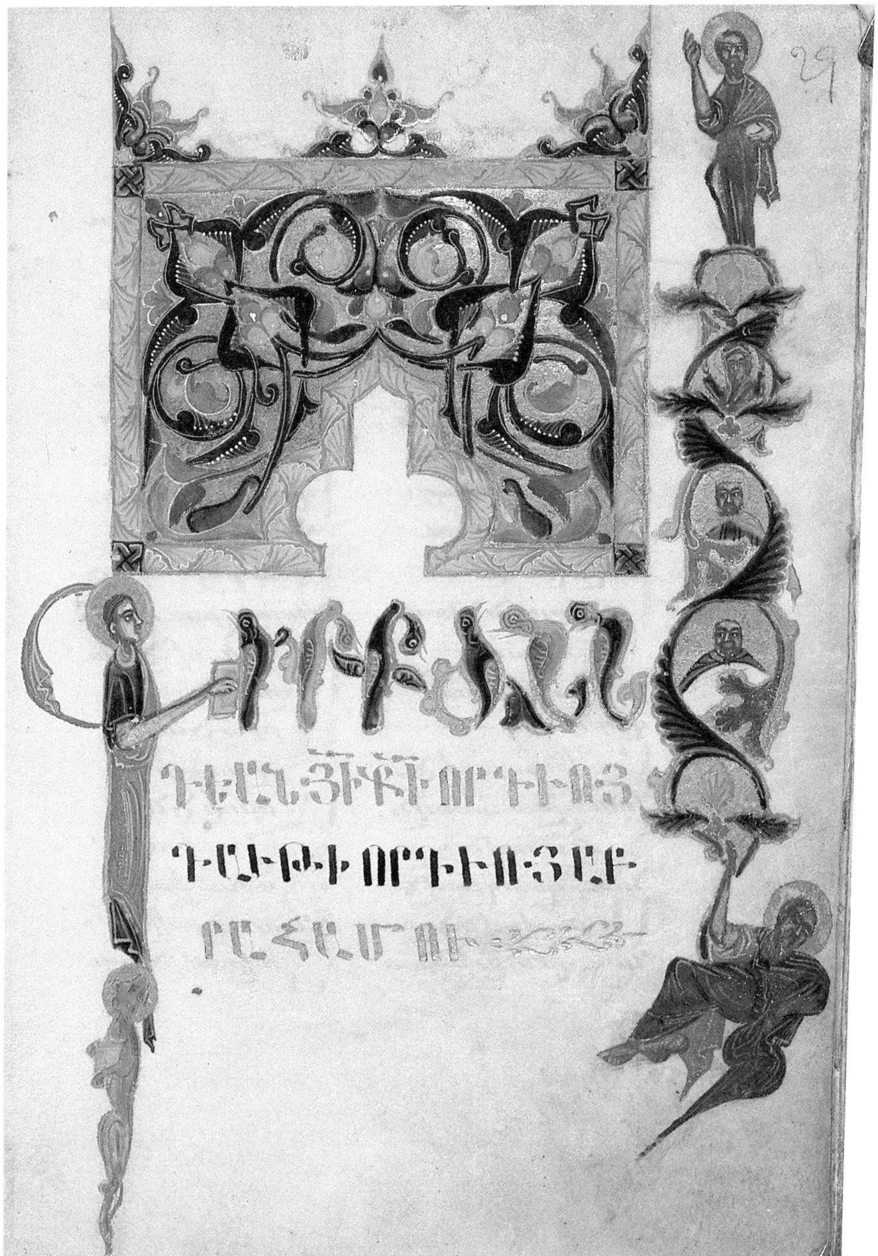

Fig. 28. *Four Gospels (MS Or.13895).*
19 × 14 cm.
fol. 29a. Headpiece of St Matthew's Gospel. The headpiece has in the outer margin a representation of the Tree of Jesse; Christ is depicted standing in a frontal pose blessing, on top of a spiral-shaped foliage forming roundels which are occupied with the busts of St Mary, David, Abraham, and the full figure of Jesse reclining at the base with one hand raised pointing to the ancestors. The symbol of St Matthew, an angel, stands upright, the wing forming the loop of the initial letter 'G' and the book forms the cross-stroke. The angel is standing on top of an outstretched lion, also holding a book and intended to be the symbol of the evangelist St Mark.
The artists of Cilicia represented the Tree of Jesse in a marginal composition on the opening page of the Gospel of St Matthew, next to the geneaology of Christ (see PLATE XIV).

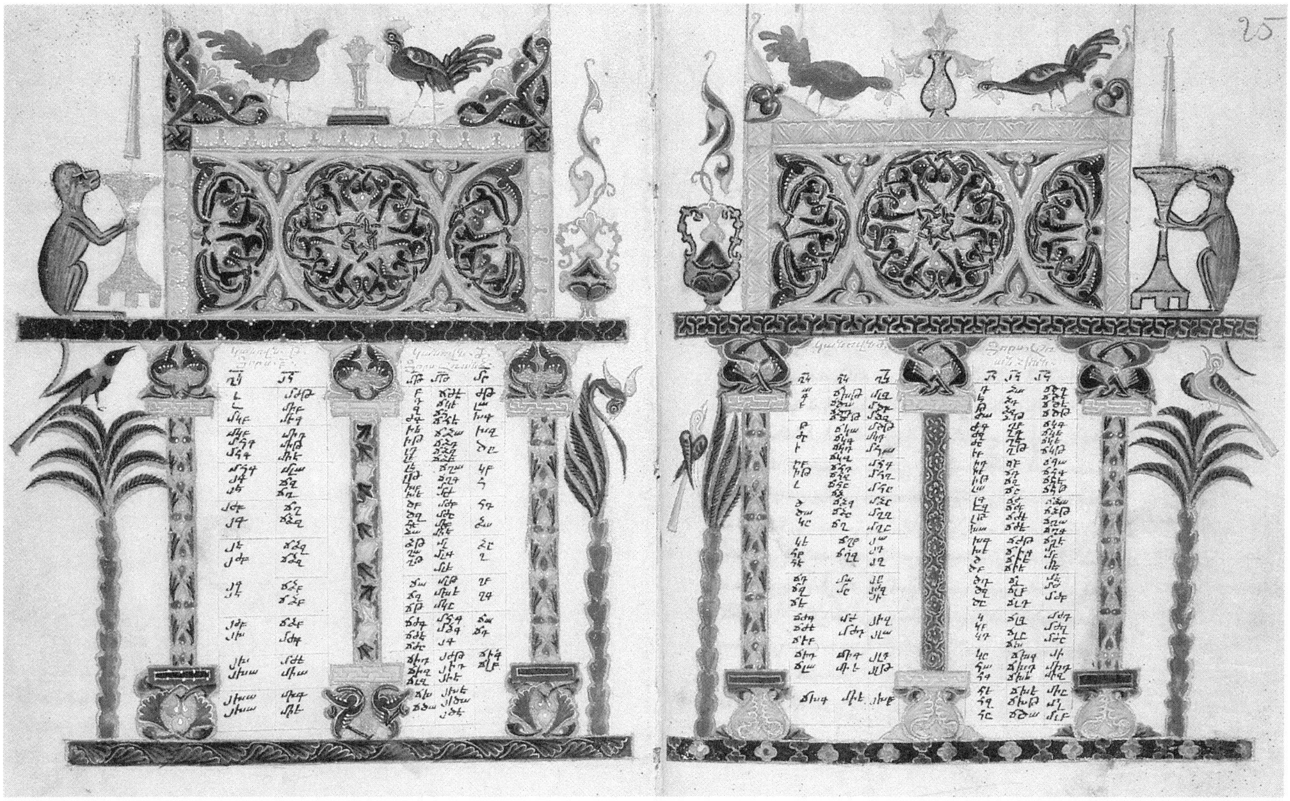

Fig. 29. *MS. Or.13895. fol. 24b–25a. Canon Tables, no. ix–x.*

has a human head, from the right of which protrudes an animal head. The figure is virtually unique to the Armenian representation of Pentecost, with the exception of three Syriac examples from the thirteenth century.

The animal figure represents one of the pagan people from a distant land; in all probability it was intended to be a dog-headed personage. In the thirteenth-century Armenian version of a sermon by Michael the Syrian, the Apostle St Andrew is spoken of as preaching the Gospel in the East in the 'land of the dog-headed people'. Moreover, the figure probably entered Armenian art in the thirteenth century because it was associated with the Mongols, who conquered Armenia and signed a treaty of alliance with the Armenian kingdom of Cilicia. King Het῾um of Cilicia visited the Mongol capital from 1253 to 1256, to pay homage. Among one of the matters related by the king which is preserved in the Armenian History of Kirakos Ganjakec῾i is a description of a nation 'beyond the Chinese' of dog-headed and hairy men. In the History of the Nation of Archers by Grigor of Akner (*d.*1272), they are described as having snouts like dogs.

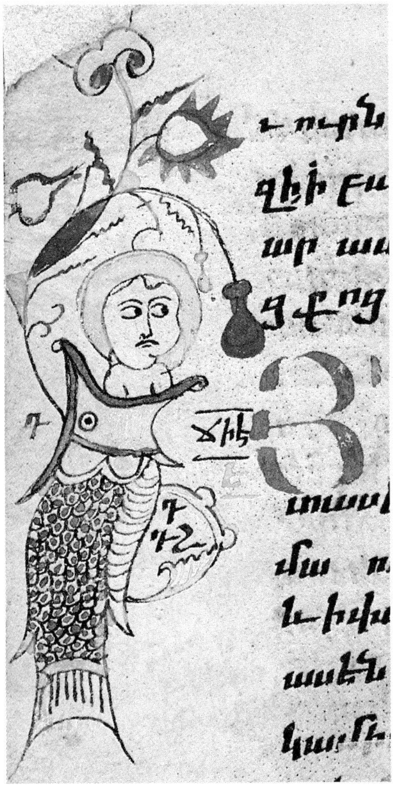

Fig. 30. *Four Gospels (MS Or.5761).*
23 × 18 cm.
fol. 33b. Jonah in the belly of the whale
(St Matthew 10:16–17).

CONCLUSION

Within the wide range of systems of Gospel illumination developed in Byzantine and East Christian art, the 'classic Armenian system' consists of a set of full-page scenes which follow the canon tables and are in turn followed by the portraits of the evangelists, sometimes the four grouped together on a single page but more commonly each preceding its respective Gospel. This arrangement, whereby the paintings are separated from the text which they are supposed to illustrate, according to Grabar 'are not so much images following a specific passage of Scripture as paintings that evoke the events described in the Gospels'.[44]

The second method of illumination found in Armenian manuscripts of the Cilician period and in manuscripts copied in Greater Armenia after the twelfth century followed the Byzantine practice of placing rectangular inserts into the text next to the passage illustrated, the result being the creation of a visual equivalent of the text, as in manuscript Or.5304 which is the work of the painter Awag (see Appendix B).

The third and possibly the most popular method of illumination in the later period is the marginal decoration – small and abbreviated images which are signs meant to recall a certain evangelical event rather than paintings which attempt to describe events.

Whichever of these methods is used it is interesting to note that each arrangement is unique in so far as the artist has consciously selected the events and episodes to which he wishes to call the reader's attention, and thus to passages that are thought to be of particular moment.[45]

Four regions are distinguishable in the development of the Armenian miniature: Greater Armenia, Armenian colonies in the Byzantine Empire; Armenian Cilicia (up to the fourteenth century); and the Armenian Diaspora, which begins after the fall of the Armenian Cilician kingdom (AD 1375), when the Armenian people were dispersed to different cities of the East and West.[46] The earlier, more oriental style, product of an indigenous Armenia closest to the artistic current, emanated from Alexandria, while that of Cilicia, developing under the influence of Greater Armenia, borrowed from Byzantine art of the twelfth and thirteenth centuries. The earlier style, closest to a purely Armenian origin, was followed in the remote regions of the country where people were least subject to outside influences.

The artists were generally monks, who created an expressive intensity in their work by emphasising stylised linear qualities in their compositions. With a simple and austere style, the artists omitted unnecessary details of landscape and background. They simplified human figures, playing down aspects of shading or contouring. Not seeking to imitate nature, they rejected the traditions of Classical art. The appeal of these manuscripts lies in their dark tones and stylised patterns, not in the achievement of realism.

In contrast, the Cilician style of painting was developed by artists schooled in the traditions of western art. The ornamental elements in Cilician manuscripts began to consist of birds or imaginary creatures painted with precision and perched on the first initial of words. Ornamentation of page margins included a wide range of motifs, sometimes taking the form of decorative floral branches or carefully drawn sets of rich and original narrative cycles. The artists used an expanded range of brilliant colours, using gold leaf without stint for the background. Contrary to Armenian artistic conventions, these artists stressed detail, rendered human forms in a more lifelike way and included background landscapes.

In concluding this essay, it is appropriate to recall the opinion of Prof. Matthews:

> 'In most of its vocabulary it is clear that the language of Armenian Gospel iconography is a language that Armenia shared with the rest of medieval Christendom. Many of the subjects and many of the compositions enjoyed a wide circulation and would have been as readily understood in Paris or Constantinople as they were in Armenia. Armenian iconography is not a separate language by itself though perhaps it could be called a distinct dialect in the common language of medieval art. To understand what is peculiarly Armenian about Armenian iconography involves pressing the language to yield its nuances of meaning.'[47]

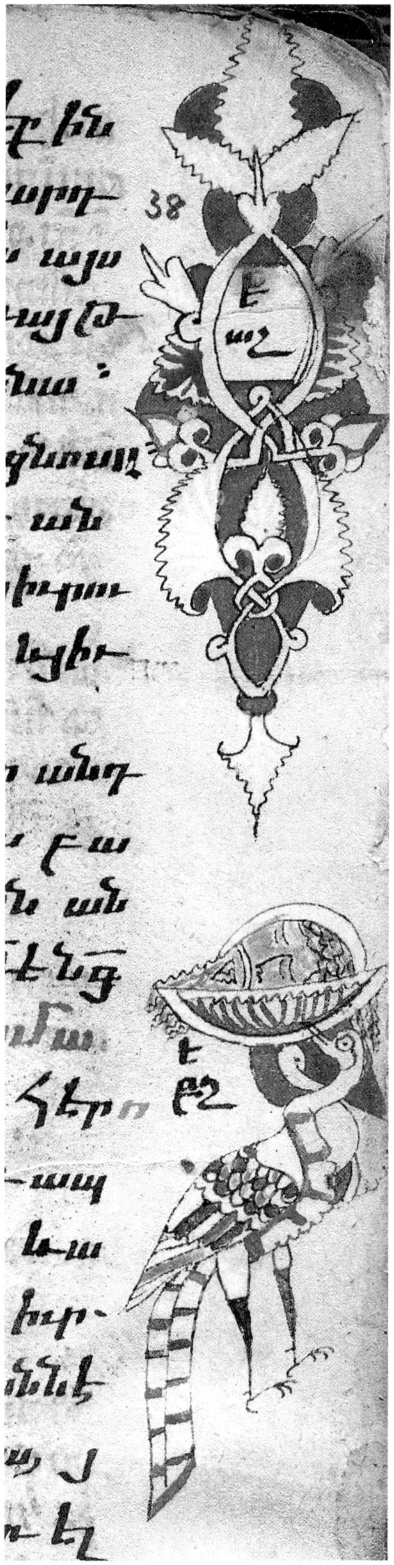

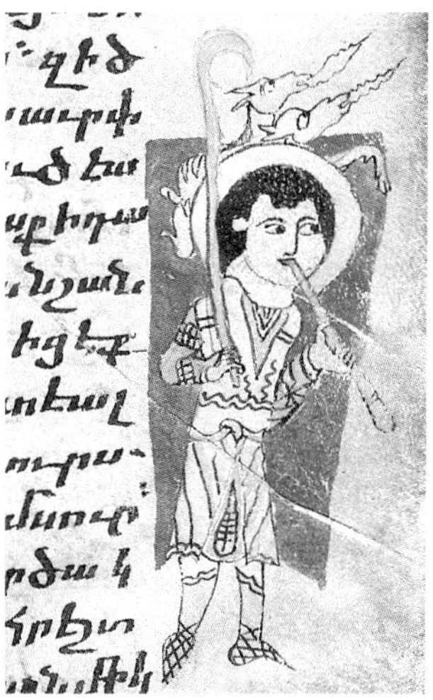

Fig. 31. (Right) *MS Or.5761. fol. 38a. The head of John the Baptist on a platter* (St Matthew 14:11).

Fig. 32. (Left) *MS Or.5761. fol. 140a. A shepherd boy playing the flute and two sheep blowing flames* (St Luke 2:8–9).

A BRIEF HISTORY OF THE ARMENIAN MANUSCRIPT COLLECTION IN THE BRITISH LIBRARY

Armenian illustrated manuscripts form one of the most important groups among the codices of the Christian East, both in their artistic quality and in the number of surviving examples. The corpus of extant Armenian manuscripts, estimated at 26000, provides an uninterrupted series of examples dating from the late ninth to the early eighteenth centuries. The largest repository of Armenian manuscripts is in the Matenadaran in Erevan, with over 13836 manuscripts including fragments. The second largest collection, consisting of 4500 manuscripts, is in the library of the Armenian Patriarchate of Jerusalem, followed by an estimated total of 4300 in the library of the Armenian Mekhitharists Order on the Island of San Lazzaro in Venice. There are 2000 in the library of the Armenian Mekhitharists in Vienna; 1000 each in the collections of New Julfa (Iran) and the Monastery of Zmmaṙ (Lebanon); 800 in the United States and smaller collections scattered throughout the libraries and museums in Moscow, Leningrad, Paris, Vatican City, Germany, Ireland, and London.

The British Library (previously the British Museum) collection of Armenian manuscripts of which 142, are described by F. C. Conybeare in his *Catalogue*,[48] though not very numerous, is thoroughly representative of the different branches of Armenian literature, and includes a number of ancient and rare works. The collection has been in progress of growth for many years, some of the volumes (as detailed below) having belonged to Sir Hans Sloane (1660–1753), Thomas Grenvill-Stowe (1755–1846), Francis Henry Egerton (*d.*1829), William Petty, 1st Marquess of Lansdowne (*d.*1805), and Robert and Edward Harley, 1st and 2nd Earls of Oxford (*d.*1724, and 1741) and Thomas Howard, 2nd Earl of Arundel (1586–1646), and Claudius James Rich (1786–1821).[49]

Arundel	*Egerton*	*Harley*	*Lansdowne*	*Rich*	*Sloane*	*Stowe*
Ar.Or.3	693	5459	1047	Add.7940	1574	Or.31
	694	5461	1048	Add.7941	4090	
	706	5558		Add.7942		
	608	7013				

As early as 1836, at the instigation of Sir Antony Panizzi (1797–1879), the Principal Librarian of the British Museum, the Trustees secured a Parliamentary grant for the purchase of all the publications issued by the press of the Mekhitharist monks on the island of S. Lazzaro, Venice 'whence had just appeared the great dictionary of the language'.[50] In June 1875 the British Museum sanctioned the preparation by Revd. Sukias Baronian of a Catalogue of the Armenian manuscripts in the British Museum. In July 1877 Dr Rieu reported back to the Trustees that the Catalogue of the Armenian manuscripts had been completed but as it was written in French and the author did not feel equal to the task of turning it into English and 'to have it translated would involve the difficulty of finding a translator and additional expenses' the approval for publication was postponed.

In November 1883 the library purchased from Baronian five manuscripts, bearing the location marks Oriental 2669, 2678, 2680, 2681, and 2682. These five and another in the Bodleian Library (Oxford) collection under Arm.d.12, also purchased from Baronian, were all once in the collection of manuscripts belonging to the 'Parish Church Council at Edessa 1868', as the imprint of a blue seal present in all the manuscripts shows.

Another source for the collection were the manuscripts of the novelist Hakob Melikʿ Hakobian, better known as Raffi. After the death of the novelist in 1888, his widow Anna Raffi with her two sons Aram and Arshak settled in London in 1895. She brought with her six manuscripts which, in May 1897, were seen and described by F. C. Conybeare. Of these, five were acquired by the British Museum and one by the University Library, Cambridge. The five forming part of the British Library's collection are MSS Or.5074, 5261, 5459, 5260, and 5462, and the University Library Cambridge MS 3429(10). The signature of the novelist is found on fol. 4a of MS 5459 and a note in the inside cover of Or.5462 states 'From the Raffi collection of manuscripts'. Add.3429(10) in the University Library of Cambridge collection sold on 4 November, 1896, has the following inscription in Armenian written by Mrs Anna Raffi 'shame on the wealthy Armenians'. The thought of having to sell her husband's manuscripts, because as she wrote in one of her letters 'I am a widow with two sons, and greatly in want of money' (4 November 1896), must have been a very painful one.

In August 1908 the Keeper of Oriental Printed Books and Manuscripts, L. D. Barnett, proposed to the Trustees that the Museum's collection of 143 Armenian manuscripts be catalogued by F. C. Conybeare, of University College Oxford, 'a scholar of distinction, for the remuneration of £5 per quarter sheet'. On 15 January 1909 F. C. Conybeare was employed to do the cataloguing and by 22 September 1913 the work was completed and published. In

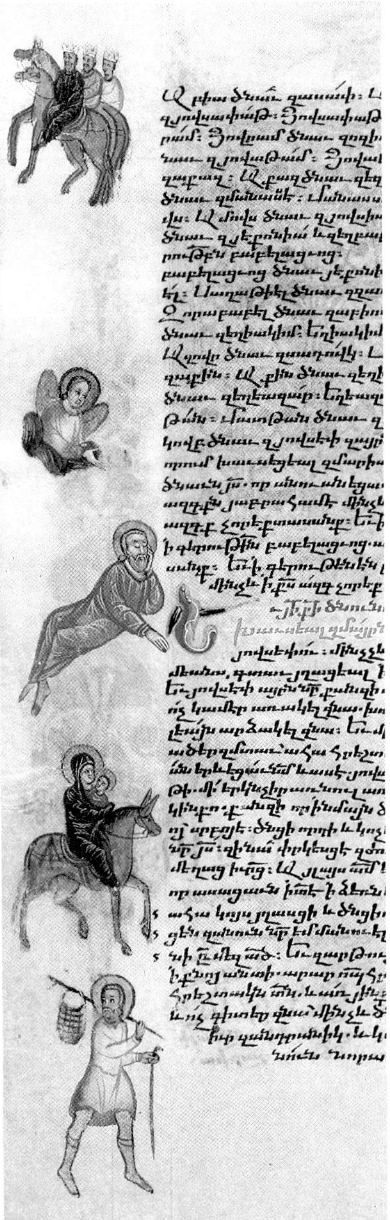

Fig. 33. *Bible (MS Or.8833).*
26 × 19 cm.
An illuminated Armenian Bible copied by Yovhannēs Lehacʿi [of Poland in AD *1646 and illuminated by the artist Łazar].*
fol. 471b. The three kings on horseback; Joseph sleeping, above him the bust of an angel; flight into Egypt – the Virgin holding the Child seated on the donkey and Joseph on foot carrying a walking stick and a basket slung over his shoulder.

the introduction to the catalogue Conybeare comments as follows: 'Some thirty years back the Revd. Dr. Baronian began a catalogue of the collection, and his uncompleted work remains, and was of much use to me. Even apart from the deep regard which during many years of intercourse I learned to feel for this high-minded and devoted son of the Church of Armenia, the guidance which his notes afforded me demands something more than a passing reference'.

In the years immediately after the publication of the Catalogue, the Armenian collection was enriched with the bequest to the Museum of the collection of the Hon Robert Curzon of Parham through Baroness Darea Zouche (Curzon inherited the title of Lord Zouche) on 13 October 1917. Lord Curzon (1810–1873) probably collected most of his manuscripts in 1838–39, during the second of his visits to Egypt, which he colourfully narrated in his *Visits to monasteries in the Levant*, or else shortly thereafter. Curzon was collecting materials for a history of writing, a list of which was published as *A catalogue of materials for writing in 1849*. In this catalogue he describes nine of the ten manuscripts which are bequeathed to the Museum on October 1917 now under numbers MSS Or.8825–8834.

Curzon concludes the description of his Armenian collection of manuscripts with the following passage: 'With the exception of the library of the Patriarchate, in the great Monastery of Echmiadzin, near Mount Ararat, which I have not visited, the largest collection of Armenian manuscripts is in the Convent of St Lazarus at Venice; but neither there, nor in the monasteries at Constantinople, Jerusalem, Erzerum, nor any of the smaller monasteries of Armenia, which I have seen, have I met with any Armenian manuscript so finely written or so splendidly illuminated as No. 4 [Or.8826, Psalter, 16th C.] and 8 [Or.8833, Bible, AD 1646], in the collection at Parham; nor have I met with any other on silk paper, like No. 1 [Or.8834, Lives of the Saints, 14th C.], though I have seen three of much higher antiquity, viz., two in uncial letters at Venice, and one in the monastery of Kuzzal Vankʿ near the sources of the Euphrates, which was written in the year 422, and for which the monks refused every offer'.[51]

In 1922 the Library acquired five manuscripts which had been in the collection of the orientalist A. G. Ellis. These comprise manuscripts Oriental 9132 to 9136, all dated from the seventeenth century.

Of the fifty manuscripts collected since the publication of the *Catalogue* twenty-six have been added since 1975, when the Armenian section was created and a curator in charge of the collections appointed. The great majority have been purchased from public auctions, principally from the sales of the Hagob Kevorkian collection. The important manuscripts Or.13654, the Gospels of Awag Vankʿ 1200/02 (Kevorkian 6), Or.13993, Breviary of King Leo II/III and Or. 13804, Psalter of Sargis Picak, were all once part of this famous collection.[52]

A *Union Catalogue of Armenian manuscripts in the United Kingdom libraries and institutions* including also descriptions of manuscripts in the British Library acquired since the year 1913 is being prepared for publication by the Calouste Gulbenkian Foundation.

Bibliography and Notes

1. Milburn, R. L. P., Rev., 'The "People's Bible": artists and commentators' in *The west from the Fathers to the Reformation*, ed. by G. W. H. Lamp (The Cambridge History of the Bible vol. 2). Cambridge, 1969, pp. 280–308; Allies Mary H, *Saint John of Damascus on Holy Images*. London, 1898, p. 19.
2. Wormald, Francis, 'Bible illustration in medieval manuscripts', *ibid*, pp. 309–337; Weitzmann, Kurt, 'Introduction' to *Age of spirituality: late antique and early Christian art, third to seventh century*. Princeton University Press, 1979, pp. xix–xxvi.
3. Nordenfalk, C., Die Spätantiken Kanontafeln. Göteborg, 1938.
4. Friend, A. M., Jr., 'The portraits of the Evangelists in Greek and Latin Manuscripts', *Art Studies* 5 (1927) and 7 (1929); Łazaryan, Vigen, 'Avetaranič῾neri patkeragrut῾yunê 13-rd dari Kilikyan manrankarč῾ut῾yan meǰ' (The portraits of the Evangelists in Armenian Cilician manuscripts), *The 2nd International symposium on Armenian art*. Erevan, 1978, vol. iv, pp. 82–94.
5. Weitzmann, Kurt, 'The narrative and liturgical Gospel illustrations' in *Studies in Classical and Byzantine manuscript illumination*, ed. by H. L. Kessler. University of Chicago Press, 1971, pp. 247–270; Kessler, Herbert L., 'Narrative representations', in *The Christian Realm*, pp. 449–456.
6. Kouymjian, Dickran, 'The Eastern case: The Classical tradition in Armenian art and the Scaenae Frons', *Byzantium and the Classical tradition*, ed. by M. Mullet & R. Scott. University of Birmingham, 1981, pp. 155–170; 'The classical tradition in Armenian art', *REA*, XV (1981), pp. 263–288, plts. i–xi; Nersessian, Der, S., 'Armenian painting' in *Armenia and the Byzantine empire*. Harvard University Press, 1945, pp. 110–136.
7. Metzger, Bruce M., *The Early versions of the New Testament: Their origin, transmission and limitations*. Oxford, 1977; Alexanian, Joseph M., 'The Armenian Gospel text from the fifth through the fourteenth centuries', in *Medieval Armenian culture*, ed. by Thomas J. Samuelian & Michael E. Stone (University of Pennsylvania Armenian Texts and Studies 6). Scholars Press, 1984, pp. 381–394; Cowe, S. P., 'A typology of Armenian Biblical manuscripts', *REA*, XVIII (1984), pp. 49–67.
8. Vrt῾anēs K῾ert῾oł, *Yałags Patkeramartic῾* printed by G. Z. Sahakian in *Sur l'intercession des saints*. Venice, 1853, pp. 325–342; Durian E. Archbishop, 'Vrt῾anēs K῾ert῾oł', *Sion*, 1–2 (1927), pp. 22–25; 61–63; French translation in Nersessian, Der, S., 'Une apologie des images du septième siècle', *Byzantion*, XVIII (1944–1945), pp. 58–87; reprinted in *Byzantine and Armenian studies*. Louvain, 1973, pp. 379–403; English translation in Kochakian, G. Revd., *Religious art in Armenian theology*. Thesis for M.D. submitted at St Vladimir's Orthodox Theological Seminary, April 1973.
9. Nersessian, Der, S., 'Image worship in Armenia and its opponents', *Armenian Quarterly*, I (1946), pp 67–81; reprinted in *Byzantine and Armenian studies*, pp. 405–415; Alexander, Paul J., 'An ascetic sect of iconoclasts in seventh century Armenia', *Late classical and medieval studies in honour of Albert M. Friend Jr.* Princeton, 1955, pp. 151–160.
10. Nersessian, Der, S., 'The date of the initial miniatures of the Etchmiadzin Gospel', *The Art Bulletin*, XV (1933), pp. 1–34; reprinted in *Byzantine and Armenian studies*, pp. 533–558.
11. Matthews, Thomas F., 'The early Armenian iconographic program of the Ēǰmiacin Gospel Erevan, Matenadaran MS 2374, olim 229)', *East of Byzantium: Syria and Armenia in the Formative period*, ed. by N. Garsoïan. Dumbarton Oaks, 1982, pp. 199–215.
12. Janashian, Mesrop, *Armenian miniature paintings*. Venice, 1966, pp. 45–72.
13. Kouymjian, Dickran, *IAA: Index of Armenian art Part I: Manuscript illuminations Fasc. I: Illuminated Armenian manuscripts to the year 1000 AD*. California State University, 1977; 'Illustrated Armenian manuscripts to the year AD 1000', *Arxeion Pontoy* (1979), pp. 249–252.
14. Izmailova, T. A., 'L'iconographie du cycle des fêtes d'un groupe de codex Arméniens d'Asie Mineure', *REA*, IV (1967), pp. 125–166.
15. Nersessian, Der, S., *The Chester Beatty Library: A catalogue of the Armenian manuscripts with an introduction on the history of Armenian art*. Dublin, 1958, p. xxi.
16. Conybeare, F. C., *Rituale Armenorum being the administration of the sacraments and the breviary rites of the Armenian Church*. Oxford, 1905, pp. 3–58.
17. Kochakian, G. Revd., English translation in *Religious art in Armenian theology*. Thesis for M.D. submitted at St Vladimir's Orthodox Theological Seminary, April 13, 1973; Nersessian, Der, S., 'Une apologie des images du septième siècle', *Byzantion*, XVII (1944–1945), pp. 58–87.
18. Nersoyan, Abp. Tiran, *Divine Liturgy of the Armenian Apostolic Orthodox Church*, with Variables, complete rubrics and commentary. London, 1984, p. 29.
19. Azaryan, L. R., *Kilikyan manrankarč῾ut῾yunê XII–XIII dd* (Cilician miniature painting in the XII–XIIIth centuries). Erevan, 1964; Nersessian, Der, S., *Manuscrits Arméniens illustres des XII, XIII et XIV siècles*. Paris 1937.
20. Abrahamyan, A. G., *Hay gri ev grč῾ut῾yan patmut῾yun* (History of Armenian alphabet and art of copying manuscripts). Erevan, 1959, pp. 268–271; Nersessian, Der, S., *The Chester Beatty Library: A catalogue of the Armenian manuscripts*. Dublin, 1958, pp. 18–21.
21. Dowsett, C. J. F., 'The Awag Vank῾ Armenian Gospels', *The British Library Journal* III, 2 (1977), pp. 139–166.

22. Kiwlēserian, Babgen, *Cʿucʿak jeṙagracʿ Łalatʿioy azgayin matenadarani hayocʿ* (Catalogue of the Armenian manuscripts in the National library at Galata). Antʿilias, 1961, MS No.6. cols 26–36.
23. Nersessian, Der, S., 'La Bible D'Erznka de l'an 1269: Jérusalem No. 1925', *Byzantine and Armenian studies*, pp. 603–609; Armenian text in *Ējmiacin* 11–12 (1966), pp. 28–39.
24. Nersessian, Der, S., *Armenian manuscripts in the Freer Gallery of Art* (with 108 plates). Washington, 1963, pp. 55–72.
25. Dowsett, C. J. F., 'An illuminated Breviary of the Armenian Orthodox Church copied for king Leo II/III', *Sotheby's catalogue, 2nd May, 1977*, lot. 177, pp. 84–85; Siwrmēian, Artawazd, Archbishop, 'Lewon III tʿagawori žamagirkʿē' (The Breviary of king Lewon III), *Hask Hayagitakan Taregirkʿ*, 2nd year (1949–50), pp. 49–57; Yovsepʿeancʿ Garegin, 'Stepʿanos Vahkaycʿi', *ibid.* pp. 58–64.
26. Sanjian, Avedis K., *A catalogue of medieval Armenian manuscripts in the United States*. University of California, 1976, pp. 582–596.
27. Yovsepʿeancʿ Garegin, 'Glajori barjr dprocʿē kam "Hamalsaran"-ē (The school or "University" of Gladjor), *Xałbakeankʿ kam Pṙošeankʿ*. Jerusalem, 1944, pp. 188–279; Avetisyan, A. N., *Haykakan manrankarčʿutʿyan Glajori dprocʿē* (The Armenian miniature school of Gladjor). Erevan, 1971; Abrahamyan, A., *Glajori Hamalsaranê* (The University of Gladjor). Erevan, 1983; Łazarosyan, A., 'Glajori hamalsarani gričʿnerê ev jeṙagrerê' (The scribes and manuscripts of the University of Gladjor), *Lraber Has.Gitutʿyunneri*, 3 (1984), pp. 58–66; 'Glajori hamalsaranum êndōrinnakvac jeṙagrer' (Manuscripts copied at the University of Gladjor), *Ējmiacin*, 11–12 (1984), pp. 56–59.
28. Korxmazyan, Emma, *Toros Taronatsi*. Erebouni, 1984; *Armenian miniatures of the 13th and 14th centuries from the Matenadaran collection Yerevan*. Leningrad, 1984, pp. 11–13; Avetisyan, A. N., *Haykakan manrankarčʿutʿyan Glajori dprocʿē*, 86–134.
29. Sanjian, Avedis K., *A catalogue of medieval Armenian manuscripts in the United States*. University of California, 1976, MS. ARM.3, pp. 81–89.
30. Nersessian, Der, S., 'Western iconographic themes in Armenian manuscripts', *Byzantine and Armenian Studies*, Louvain, 1973, pp. 611–630.
31. Nersessian, Der, S., *The Chester Beatty Library: A catalogue of the Armenian manuscripts*, MS 559, pp. 31–33; Four full-page miniatures signed by the artist Tʿoros *sarkawag* belonging to this same manuscript in the collection of H. Hazarian were sold at Sotheby's on 26th November, 1985. See *Western manuscripts and miniatures*, lot. 142.
32. Zakʿaryan, Lilitʿ, 'Awag całkoł' (The painter Awag), *Ējmiacin*, 7–8 (1985); *Awag*. Erebouni, 1984.
33. Avetisyan, A. N., *Haykakan manrankarčʿutʿyan Glajori dprocʿē*, pp. 140–151.
34. Conybeare, F. C., *A catalogue of the Armenian manuscripts in the British Museum*. London, 1913, MS 16, pp. 27–28; Nersessian, Der, S., *The Chester Beatty Library . . .*, pp. xxxii, n.1, 57, n.2, 75, n.1.
35. Vardanyan, V. M., *Vaspurakani Arcrunyacʿ tʿagavorutʿyunê 908–1021* (The Arcruni kingdom of Vaspurakan 908–1021). Erevan, 1969.
36. Hakobyan, H. H., *Vaspurakani manrankarčʿutʿyunê* (The miniature school of Vaspurakan), Vol. I & II. Erevan, 1976, 1982; *Haykakan manrankarčʿutʿyun Vaspurakan: Armenian miniature Vaspurakan Album*. Erevan, 1978.
37. Nerses Šnorhali, *Meknutʿiwn surb Awetaranin or êst Mattʿēosi* (Commentary on the Holy Gospel of St Matthew). Constantinople, 1825. The commentary up to Chapter V: vv. 17 was by the author but the rest was written by Yovhannēs Erznkacʿi–Corcorecʿi; modern transl. by Garegin Xačʿaturian in *Šołakatʿ* Oct–Nov. (1952), pp. 290–296; Y. Kiwrtean (Kudian), 'Meknutʿiwn xoranacʿ Awetaranin asacʿeal teaṙn Nersisi Šnorhalwoy' (Commentary on the ten canon tables composed by Nerses Šnorhali), *Bazmavep*, 3–4 (1973), pp. 419–437; prints the 1825 classical Armenian text with study.
38. Evans, H., 'Canon tables as indication of teacher-pupil relationships in the career of Tʿoros Roslin', in *Medieval Armenian culture*, ed. T. J. Samuelian, pp. 282–290; Mahe J.-P., 'Siramargn u skahê haykakan Awetaranneri xorannerum' (The peacock and the chalice in the canon table of Armenian Gospels), *Patma-Banasirakan Handēs* 1 (1986), pp. 106–112.
39. Nersessian, Der, S., *Manuscrits Arméniens illustrés des XII, XIII et XIV siècles*, pp. 58–61; Nersessian, Der. S., & Mekhitarian, A., *Armenian miniatures from Isfahan*. Brussels. Editeurs d'Art, 1986; Kiwrtean, Y. [Kurdian], *Xizani dprocʿin gričʿnern u manrankaričʿnerê ew irencʿ yišatakarannerê* (The Armenian manuscripts and miniatures of Khizan). Paris. Imp. Araxes, 1951.
40. Korxmazyan, E. M., *Armyanskaya miniatyura Khrima* (The miniature school of Crimea). Erevan, 1978, pp. 77–85; Gevorgyan, A., 'Armyanskii miniatyurist XVII veka Nikogos tsakharar' (Armenian miniaturist of the XVIIth century Nikołos *całkarar*), *Lraber Hask.Gitutʿyunneri*, 3 (1970), pp. 89–96; plts. i–iv.
41. Kouymjian, Dickran, 'The problem of the zoomorphic figure in the iconography of Armenian Pentecost: A preliminary report', in *Primo Simposio Internazionale Di Arte Armena*. Venezia, 1978, pp. 403–407, fig. 1–9.

42. Tašean, Yakovbos, *Cʿucʿak jeṙagracʿ matenadaranin Mxitʿareancʿ i Vienna* (Catalogue of the Armenian manuscripts in the Mekhitarist convent in Vienna). Vienna, 1895, MS 319, pp. 761–763.
43. Duchesne, Aîné, *Voyage d'un iconophile revue des principaux cabinets d'estampes, bibliothèques et musées d'Allemagne, de Hollande et d'Angleterre.* Paris, 1834; this manuscript is listed among the collection of Cabinet de M. Brisard of Gand, pp. 326–327; the same description is repeated in *Catalogue de la magnifique et précieuse collection de Livres, manuscrits, dessins et estampes formant le Cabinet de Mr. R. Brisart, Rentier, a Gand.* Gand, [1849], pp. ix; The Manuscript was bought through Michelmore's in June 1934 for the 4th Marquess of Bute.
44. Grabar, André, *Christian iconography: A study of its origins.* Princeton University Press, 1968, p. 89.
45. Weitzmann, Kurt, 'The Narrative and liturgical Gospel Illustrations' in *Studies in Classical and Byzantine manuscripts illumination*, ed. by H. L. Kessler. University of Chicago Press, 1971.
46. Janashian Mesrop, *Armenian miniature paintings*, pp. 10–11.
47. Matthews, Thomas F., 'Gospel iconography in Greater Armenia' [to be published].
48. Conybeare, F. C., *A catalogue of the Armenian manuscripts in the British Museum.* London, 1913.
49. Arundell, Esdaile, *The British Museum Library: a short history and survey.* London, 1948, p. 310.
50. Reference to the publication in 1836 of *Nor Baṙgirkʿ haykazean lezui* (New Armenian dictionary). This decision is well supported by completeness of the collection as regards to publications originating in Venice; see Nersessian, V., *Catalogue of early Armenian books 1512–1850.* The British Library, 1980.
51. Curzon, Robert, Hon., *Catalogue of materials for writing, early writings on tablets, and stones, rolled and other manuscripts and oriental manuscript books in the library of the Hon. Robert Curzon Parham in the county of Sussex.* London, 1849, pp. 16–18.
52. *See* List of studies published on the British Library's Armenian manuscripts (pp. 51–52 below).

List of studies published on the British Library's Armenian manuscripts

General

Conybeare, F. C., *A catalogue of the Armenian manuscripts in the British Museum*, London, 1913.

Buchthal, Hugo and Otto, Kurz, *A hand list of illuminated oriental Christian manuscripts*, London: The Warburg Institute, 1942. Pp. 86–88.

Pearson, J. D., *Oriental manuscripts in Europe and North Africa*, Switzerland: IDCC, 1965. Pp. 172–173.

Rhodes, Erroll F., *An annotated list of Armenian New Testament manuscripts*, Japan: Rikkyo (St Paul's) University, 1959, Pp. 11–17, Nos. 74–109.
The Book through five thousand years, edited by H. D. I. Vervliet, London: Phaidon, 1973. Pp. 106–107.
The Christian Orient, edited by G. E. Marrison, London: The British Library, 1978, Pp. 57–68.

Nersessian, Vrej, *Armenian manuscript illumination*: 12 colour slides with a commentary, London: British Museum publications, 1978.

Individual manuscripts

Brisart, R., *Catalogue de la magnifique et précieuse collection de livres, manuscrits, dessins et estampes formant le cabinet de Mr. R. Brisart, Rentier, a Gand.* Gand: Van der Meersch, [1849]. Pp. ix and 1 [Or.14161].

Christie's, *Early printed books and manuscripts*, 1 June 1977, lot. 192, pp. 80–81 [Or.13808].
Valuable early printed books and manuscripts, 30 January 1980, lot. 228, p. 77 [Or.13933].

Conybeare, F. C., 'The Euthalian apparatus in the British Museum Armenian manuscripts Add.19730', *Journal of Philology*, XXIII (1895), pp. 241–259.

Conybeare, F. C., 'Four Armenian tracts on the structure of the human body' in *Studies in the history and method of science*, ed. Charles Singer, vol. II (1921), pp. 359–384. [Or.6798, Or.3712].

Curzon, Robert, Hon., *Catalogue of materials for writing, early writings on tablets and stones, rolled and other manuscripts and oriental manuscript books in the library of the Hon. Robert Curzon Parham in the county of Sussex.* London: William Nicol, 1849. Pp. 16–18 [Or.8825 to Or.8834. Ten were from his collection though only nine is listed in his catalogue].

Dowsett, C. J. F., 'An illuminated Armenian Menologium', *The British Museum Quarterly*, XXIV, 3–4 (1961), 87–94 [Or.12550].

Dowsett, C. J. F., 'The Awag Vankʻ Armenian Gospels', *The British Library Journal*, III, 2 (1977), 139–166 [Or.13654].

Duchesne, Aîné, *Voyage d'un Iconophile revue des principaux cabinets d'estampes, bibliothèques et musées d'Allemagne, de Hollande et d'Angleterre.* Paris: Heideloff et Campe, 1834. Pp. 326–327 [Or.14161].

Grigorean, Mesrop, Revd., 'Hayerēn jeṙagirner Anglia' (Armenian manuscripts in England), *Handēs Amsōreay* (1961), 495–510; reprinted in Ōskean, H., *Cʻucʻak jeṙagracʻ or i Handēs Amsōreay* (Catalogue of manuscripts printed in Handēs Amsōreay), Vienna: Calouste Gulbenkian Foundation, 1976. Pp. 335–364 [Or.12550].

Grigorean, S. Tēr, 'Haykakan hin jeṙagirner Lontoni Britanakan tʻangaranum' (Ancient Armenian manuscripts in the British Museum, London), *Bazmavep* (1923), 5–7; 66–69; 101–104; 135–138 [Add.19727, Or.81, Or.5737].

Hapēšean, H., 'Sałmosaran gruac Lewon III tʻagawori hamar' (A Psalter copied for king Lewon IIIrd, 1283), *Handēs Amsōreay*, 36 (1922), 139–155 [Or.13804]. *See* Sotheby's.

Kiwlēserian, Babgēn, *Cʻucʻak jeṙagracʻ Łalatʻioy azgayin matenadarani hayocʻ* (Catalogue of Armenian manuscripts in the national library at Galata), Lebanon: Antʻilias, 1961. MS No. 6, cols. 26–36 [Or.13654].

Kiwrtean, Y., [Kudian] 'Yaweluac'akan telekut'iwnner Britanakan T'angarani hayerēn jeṙagirneru masin' (Additional information on the Armenian manuscripts of the British Museum), *Sion*, 45 (1971), 56–57. [MSS Add. Add.21932; Add.19727; Harl.5461; Or.2678; Or.81; Or.2679; Add.19730; Add.18549; Or.2283; Or.5626; Or.2680; Add.15411; Or.2681; Or.5304; Or.2668; Or.5449; Or.5671; Add.19549; Or.5737; Add.11857; Or.2682; Add.27300; Or.2669; Add.23900; Or.5088 and Or.2615].

Macler, Frederic, 'Notice d'un Tetraevangile Armenian de la collection Lanna (Prague)', *Revue des etudes Armeniennes*, VI, 2 (1926), pp. 27–31.

Mat'evosyan, Artašes, 'Čanaparhac'oyc' J̌ułayec'i Petrosi ordi Hakobi' (Itinerary of Petros of Julfa son of Hakob), *Banber Matenadarani*, 8 (1967), 285–289 [Sloane 4090(17)].

Muyldermans, J., 'À propos d'un feuillet de manuscrit arménien (Brit. Mus., Cod. arm 118)', *Le Muséon*, 65 (1952), 11–16 [Or.5459].

Nersessian, Vrej, 'Hayeren nor jeṙagrer Angliayum' (New Armenian manuscripts in England), *Banber Matenadarani*, 13 (1980), 334–339 [Or.13933, and Or.13941].

Nersessian, Vrej, 'A unique lexicographical manuscript' in the British Library, *Patma-Banasirakan Handēs*, 4 (1983), pp. 76–81 [Or.9136].

Rogers, J. M., *Islamic art and design 1500–1700*, London: British Museum Publications, 1983. [Or.6471, 18549, pp. 41–44; and Or.14101, p.84].

Siwrmēian, Artawazd, Archbishop, 'Lewon III t'agawori žamagirk'ē' (The Breviary of Lewon III), *Hask Hayagitakan taregirk'* 2nd year (1949–50), pp. 49–57 [Or.13993].
Mayr c'uc'ak hayerēn jeṙagrac' Ewropayi masnawor hawak'umneru = Grand catalogue des manuscrits Arméniens des collections particulières d'Europe. Paris. Imp. Artistique, 1950, pp. 36–42 [Or.13993].

Sotheby's, *Catalogue of important oriental manuscripts and miniatures*: The property of The Hagop Kevorkian Fund, 2 May 1977, lot. 175, 81–82 [Or.13804; lot. 177, pp. 84–85, Or.13993].
Catalogue of fine oriental miniatures, manuscripts, 23 April 1979, lot. 182, pp. 146–148 [Or.13895].
Catalogue of fine oriental miniatures, manuscripts and printed books, 27 April 1982, lot. 300, pp. 137–140 [Or.14101].
Catalogue of the Bute collection of forty-two illuminated manuscripts and miniatures, 13 June 1983, lot. 40, pp. 149–151 [Or.14161].
Catalogue of important manuscripts and miniatures: The property of The Hagop Kevorkian Fund, 7 April 1975, lot. 197, pp. 97–99 [Or.13654].

Yovsep'eanc', Garegin I, *Yišatakarank' jeṙagrac' hator I (V daric' minč'ew 1250t')* (Colophons of Armenian manuscripts from the Vth century to 1250). Lebanon: Ant'ilias, 1951, No. 290, cols. 637–48 [Or.13654].

Yovsep'eanc', Garegin I, 'Step'anos Vahkayc'i' (Step'anos of Vahka), *Hask Hayagitakan Taregirk'* 2nd year (1949–50), pp. 58–64 [Or.13993].

THE PLATES

PLATE I

FOUR GOSPELS (MS Or.81)

Manuscript on vellum, 375 leaves, in thirty-one quires of twelve folios; each quire is numbered in upper right-hand corner. Size 22 × 16 cm. The text is written in double columns of eighteen lines in regular and neat *erkatʿagir* or uncial hand.

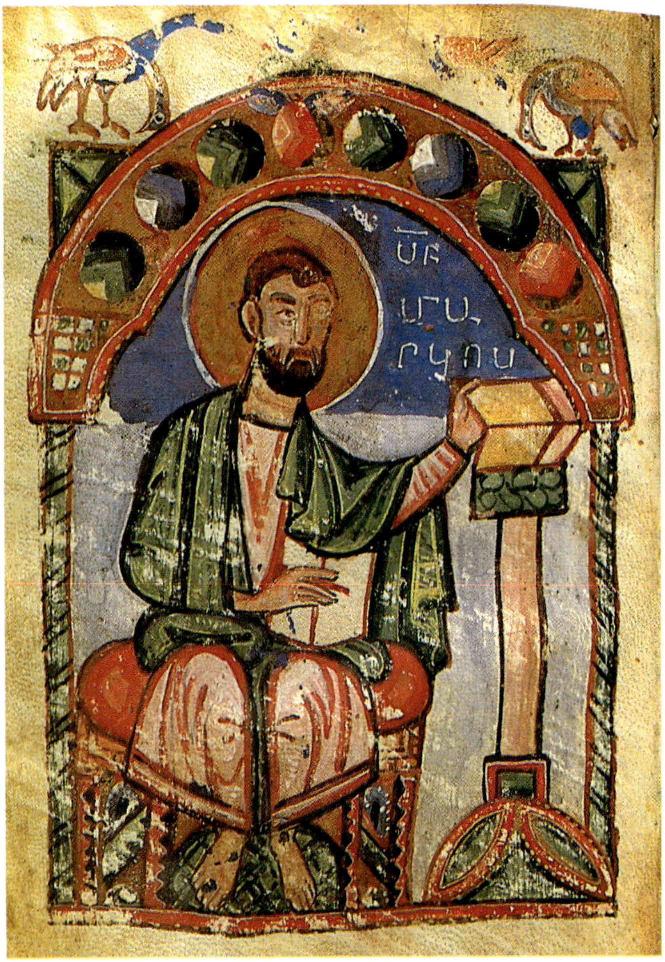

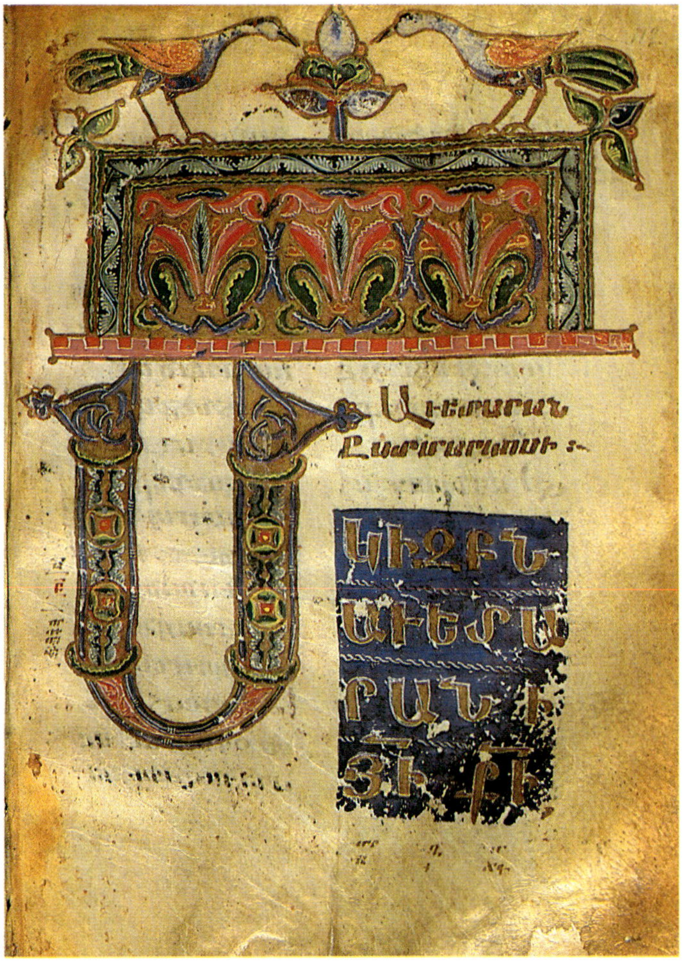

Left: fol.111b. Portrait of St Mark
St Mark seated under an ornate arch inscribed in the rectangular frame with two birds above the rectangle. The figure of the Evangelist is pleasing. He is a bearded man, garbed in the Byzantine manner, wearing over the alb a green chasuble, which covers his shoulders and fall to his knees. He is holding in his left hand his gospel, and the right hand is raised holding the book placed on the lectern.

Right: fol.112a. Headpiece of St Mark's Gospel
The headpiece of St Mark is a rectangle of small size, decorated with floral motifs with two birds standing at the sides of a floral motif. The festooned letter 'S', almost as tall as the page, fills the left margin with the rest of the text written on a blue background in large uncials. The headpieces are relatively simple and the range of ornamental motifs is fairly restricted compared with the decorations of the luxury manuscripts written at Skevra in the last decade of the 12th century.

Four Gospels (MS Or.5626)

Manuscript on vellum, 344 folios, in twenty-eight quires, all of twelve leaves. Size 15·8 × 10 cm. The text is in a clear, middle-size *bolorgir*, written in double columns of nineteen lines each.

PROVENANCE The colophon (fols. 100, 160b, 343b) indicates that the MS was written in the Armenian era 731 [i.e. AD 1282] in the monastery of Drazark by the scribe Barseł.

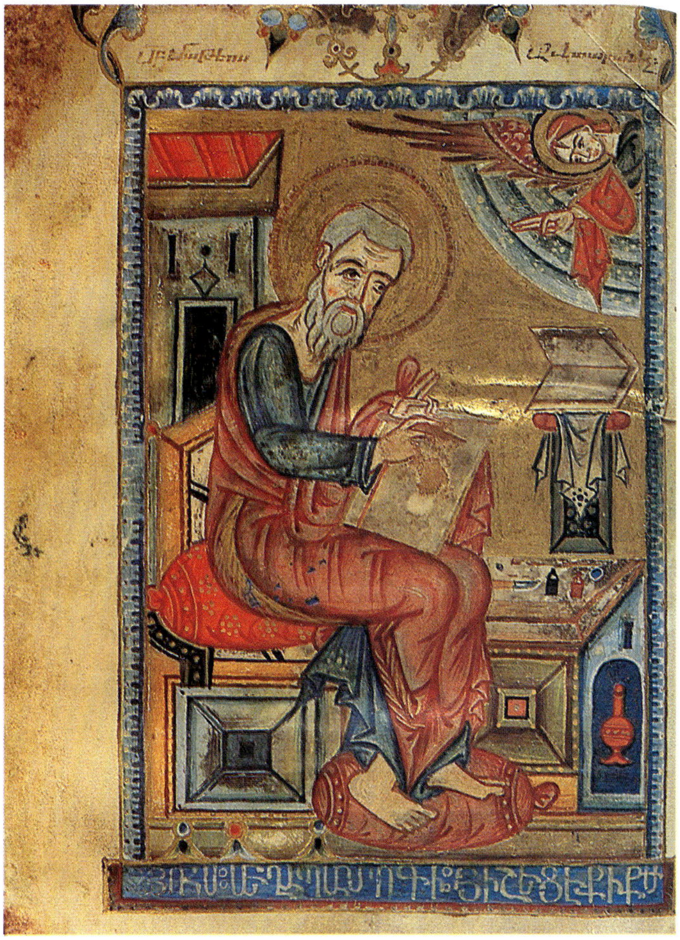

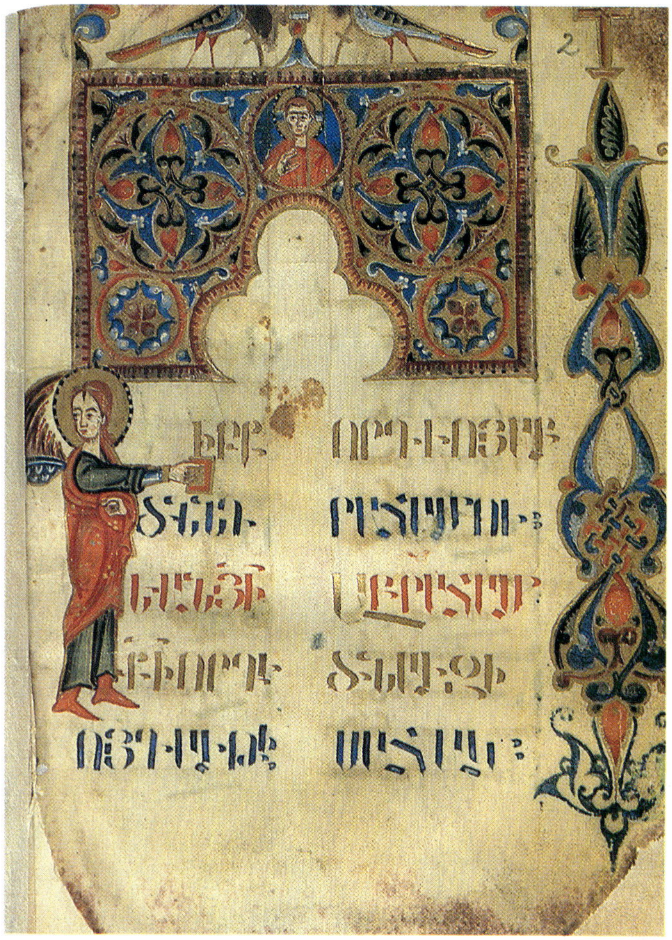

Left: fol.1b. Portrait of St Matthew
St Matthew seated in graceful pose, bending forward as he writes on the open book resting on his knees, clad in dark-blue tunic with lilac mantle, the loose end of which is brought forward by the left hand which holds the open book, and it ends in a knot. The draperies are modeled by subtle gradations of colour, especially the folds which are tucked under the knee and fall in triangular pleats.

Right: fol.2a. Headpiece of St Matthew's Gospel
The headpiece of Matthew's Gospel is ⊓-shaped with multifoil opening into the rectangle filled with intricate foliate scrolls painted in blue against gold ground; in the centre of the rectangle Christ's portrait in a disk and above two birds stand at the sides of a vase. The large ornament in the margin is crowned with a cross. The initial of Matthew is formed by his symbol – a full-figure winged angel holding a book, and the remaining text is written in alternating lines of gold, blue, and red capital letters.

PLATE III

Four Gospels (MS Or.13654)

Manuscript on vellum, 384 folios, regathered, probably in the seventeenth century, into twenty-one fascicles. Size 37 × 29 cm. The text is arranged on the page in double column, with seventeen lines per column, written in large, thick, upright *erkatʿagir*.

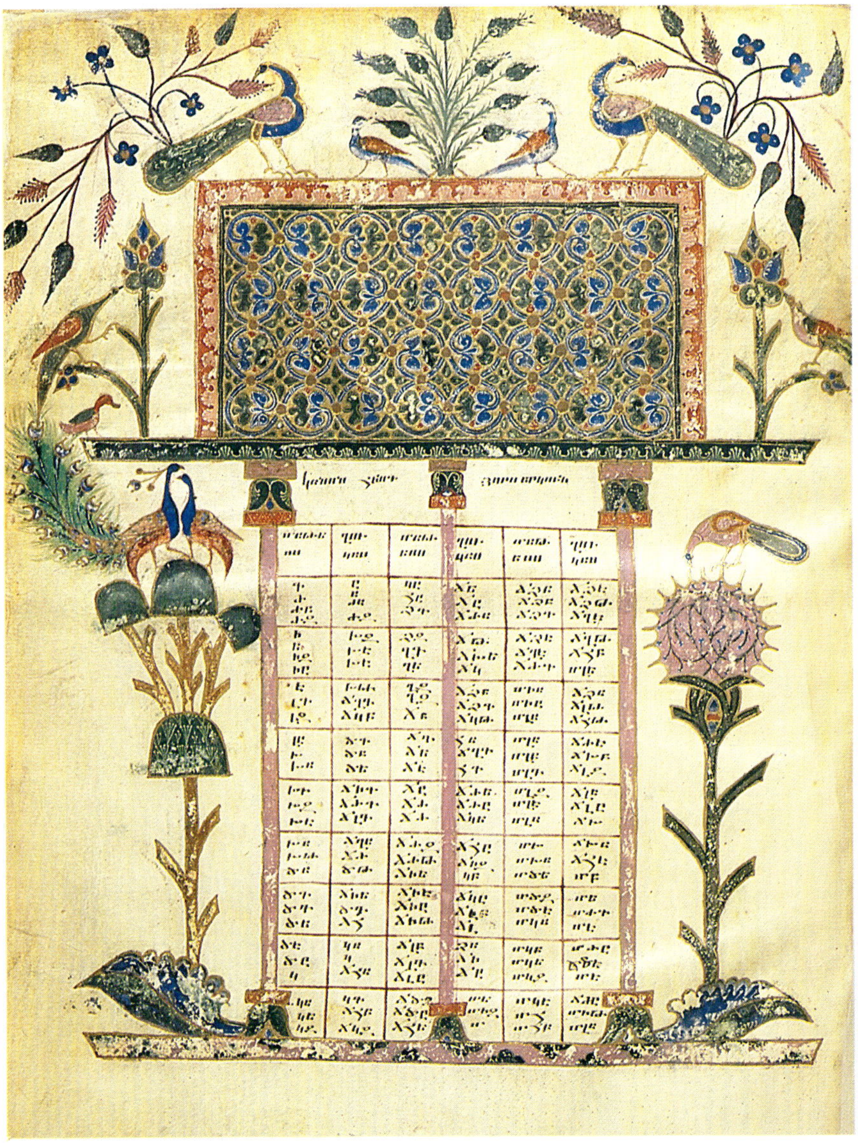

Fol.5b. The Eusebian Canon Table, no. V

The concordance numbers enclosed between coloured architectural columns flanked by imaginary trees and plants surmounted by numerous birds, beneath large headpieces. Their forms are stylised, but the different species can be recognised and their attitudes are well observed. According to the symbolical interpretation of the ornaments the fifth canon represents Noah's Ark.

Fol.229a. Headpiece of St John's Gospel

The eagle of St John is represented at the base of the decorated capital 'I' with halo and book placed on its wings.

The place assigned to the symbols of the evangelists in manuscript is not consistent. The artists of Greater Armenia usually represented each symbol next to the first letter of the Gospel, or, less frequently, in the lunette of the headpiece (Fig. 4). When the symbol of the evangelist does not form the initial of the Gospel (Fig. 6) it is usually introduced inside the frame of the portrait of the evangelist (Fig. 23). This type of composition occurs in Byzantine manuscripts of the eleventh and twelfth centuries.

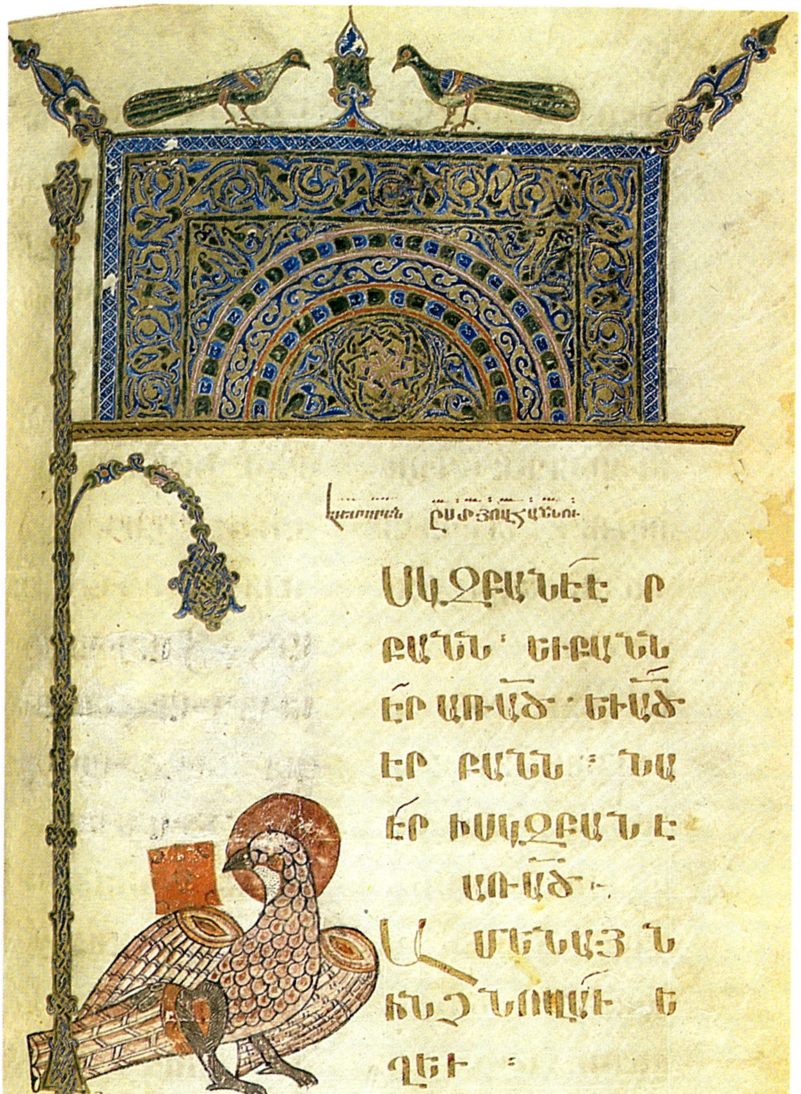

FOUR GOSPELS AND THE VISION OF THE PROPHET ISAIAH (MS Or.10960)

Manuscript on paper, 202 folios, in partly signed quires numbered i–vi of twelve leaves. The rest of the gatherings are unnumbered. Size 24·5 × 16 cm. Text written in clear *bolorgir*, in two columns of twenty-nine lines each.

PROVENANCE There is no precise indication of the place where the manuscript was copied, or its date. The colophon (fol. 201) records that the manuscript was presented by King Het῾um II (1289–1307) to Marshal Ōšin, Lord of Lambron, who has added his own memorial as owner of the manuscript 'in the Armenian era 744' [i.e. 1295]. The scribe of the manuscript is T῾oros Vahkayc῾i a compatriot of Step῾annos Vahkayc῾i.

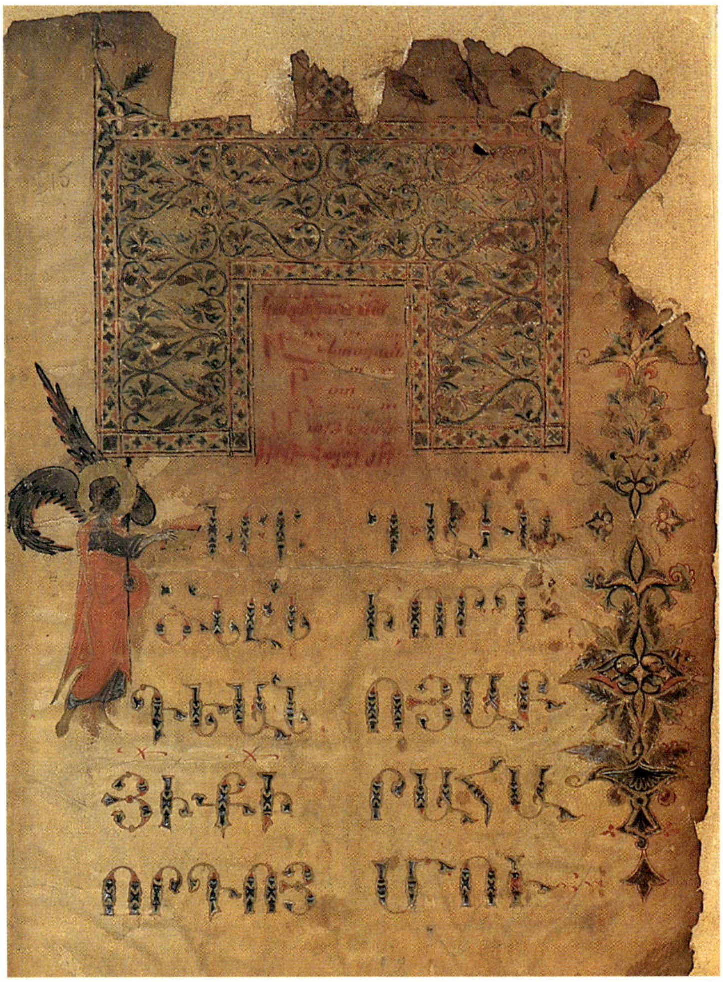

Fol.1a. Headpiece of St Matthew's Gospel
This is the most attractive of the five headpieces preserved in the manuscript. An intricate interlacement of leaves fills the headpiece, painted in green against gold ground. The full-length page ornate marginal comprises an interlacing foliate motif crowned with an ornamental cross. The initial letter of St Matthew's gospel 'G' is an elegantly executed angel with wings and nimbus wearing a red tunic. The out-stretched hand holding a book forms the horizontal arm of the letter and in the other hand she holds a staff. The remaining text in five lines in double columns is written in decorative uncials in gold outline, filled in blue and red.

The New Testament (MS Add.18549)

Manuscript on vellum, 314 folios, in twenty-six signed quires of twelve leaves each. Size 22.5 × 16 cm. The writing is an elegant medium-sized *bolorgir*, in double columns of twenty-nine lines each.

The illuminations belong to two distinct periods. The headpieces (fols. 4, 44, 71, 113), marginal arabesques, birds, decorative letters, and gold uncials were done by the scribe and artist Stepʿannos Vahkaycʿi in 1280 at Sis, the capital of Cilicia. Stepʿannos was one of the pupils of Bishop Yovhannēs, the younger brother of King Hetʿum who had set up an important scriptorium at the monastery of Gr̃ner.

The pictures of the saints that adorn the margins of the Acts of the Apostles and the Epistles, the portraits of the evangelists and of Peter and Paul were added by Mesrop of Khizan in 1618 at New Julfa (Isfahān), who several years earlier in 1608 had illustrated British Library's MS Or.5737 (see p. 35).

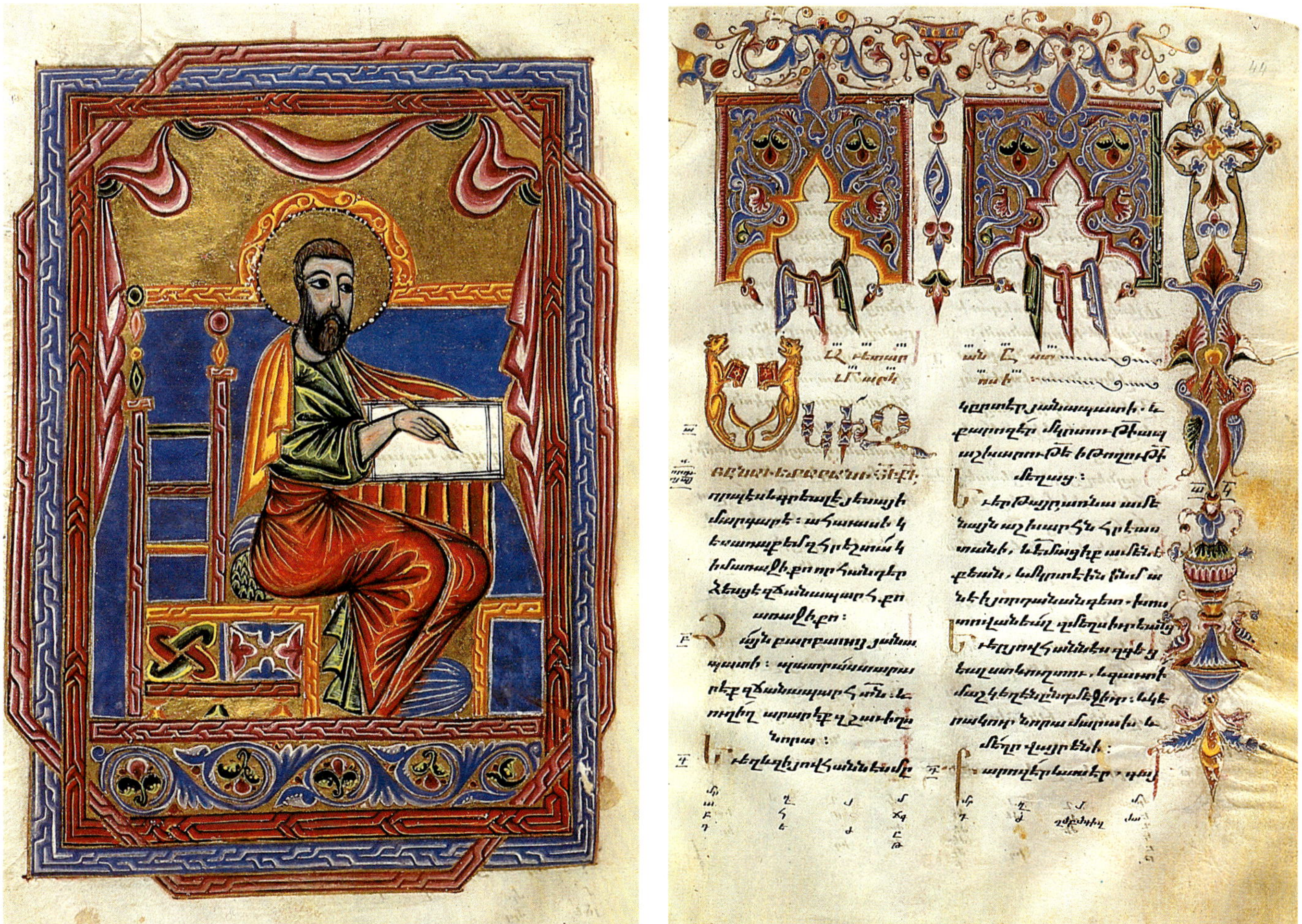

Fols.43b–44a. Portrait and headpiece of St Mark's Gospel

Four Gospels (MS Add.15411)

Manuscript on fine vellum, 312 folios, in twenty-six quires of twelve leaves each. Size 13 × 9·5 cm. The canon tables at the beginning of the book occupy nine folios and are not counted into the quires. The text is written in double columns of twenty lines each, in a neat *bolorgir* hand.

PROVENANCE The manuscript was copied in the famous University of Gladjor by the scribe Koriwn in AD 1321 for the priest Martiros. Like Add. MS 18,549 (see p. 36) this manuscript was also owned by a wealthy merchant of New Julfa Tēr Petros and his family, who had the manuscript repaired in AD 1621.

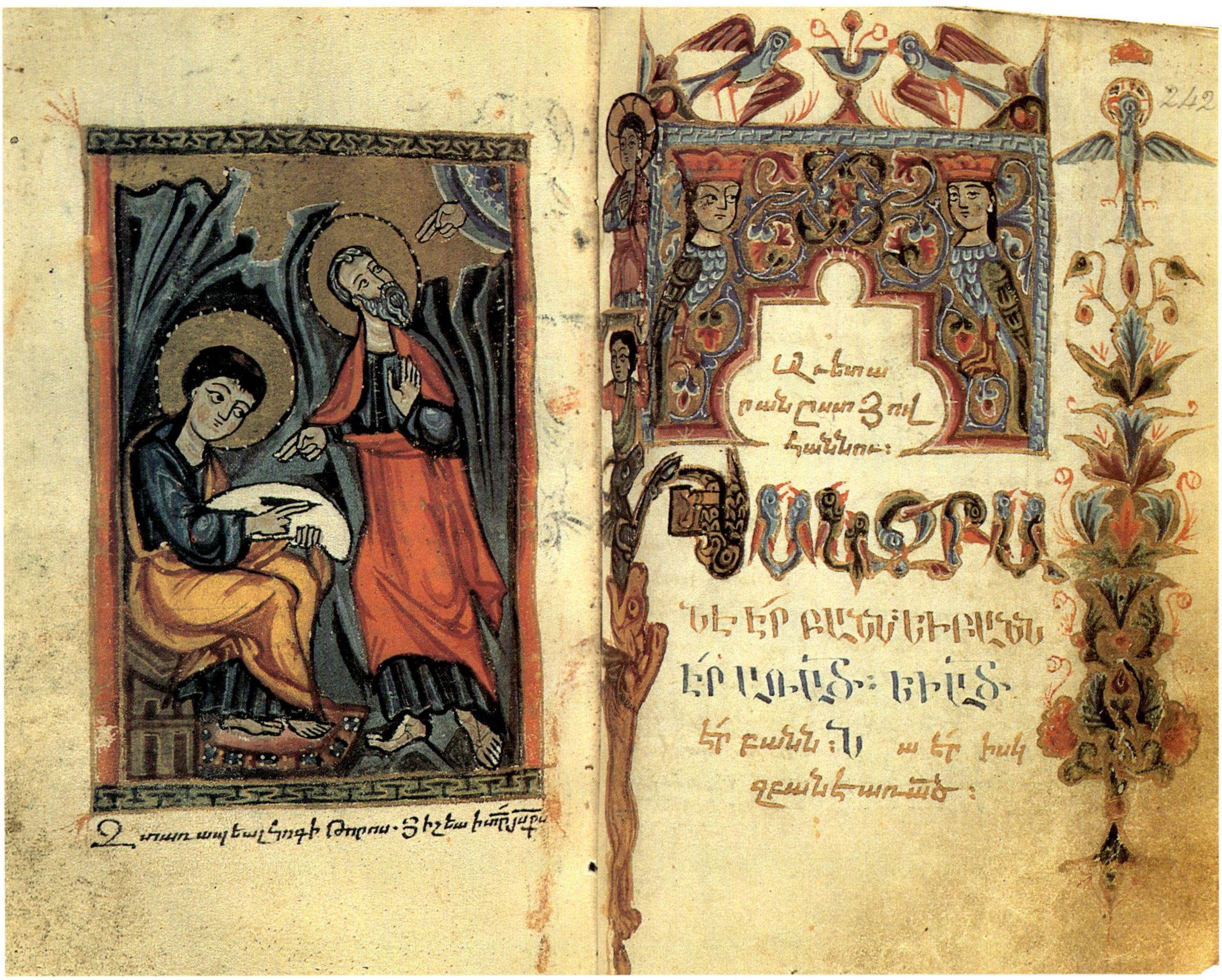

The artist of the illuminations of this manuscript is Tʿoros Taronacʿi, the foremost artist of the school of Gladjor. He has left his signature beneath the portraits of St Matthew (fol. 9b) and St John (fol. 241b); 'Ztar̄apeal hogi Tʿoros yišea i tēr Ys Kʿs [i.e. Yisus Kʿristos].

Fols.241b–242a. (Opposite) Portrait and headpiece of St John's Gospel
The portrait of the evangelist precedes each of the Gospels. The fourth evangelist is depicted standing in front of a rocky mountain, and dictating to his disciple Prochoros who is represented seated.

The initial of the Gospel of John, instead of being composed only by an eagle, Tʿoros Tar̄onacʿi has used all four symbols for this letter. The eagle forms the loop of the Armenian letter 'I'; the vertical bar is composed by the lion, the ox, the angel, standing one above the other, and the uppermost figure – the angel – supports with raised arms the enthroned Christ. The first line of the text is written in bird capitals.

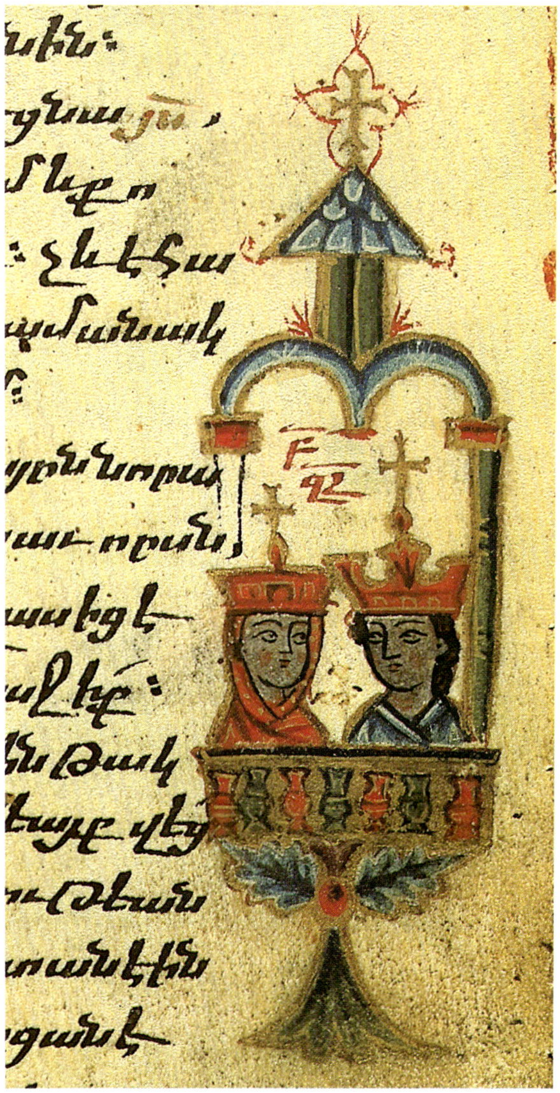

Fol.246a. (Right) The bride and groom sitting under a canopy, with seven jars of water (John 2:5–6).

The New Testament (MS Or.5304)

Manuscript on fine vellum, seventy-five folios, (incomplete at the end), the quires are not numbered. Size 22 × 16 cm. The text is written in small, neat *bolorgir*, in double columns of forty-eight lines each.

PROVENANCE The name of the painter, which allows us to date the manuscript accurately, is contained in a brief memorial written at the end of the Letter of Eusebius. This name and the style of the miniatures leave no doubt that the illustrations are the work of the painter Awag who was active between the years 1329 and 1358.

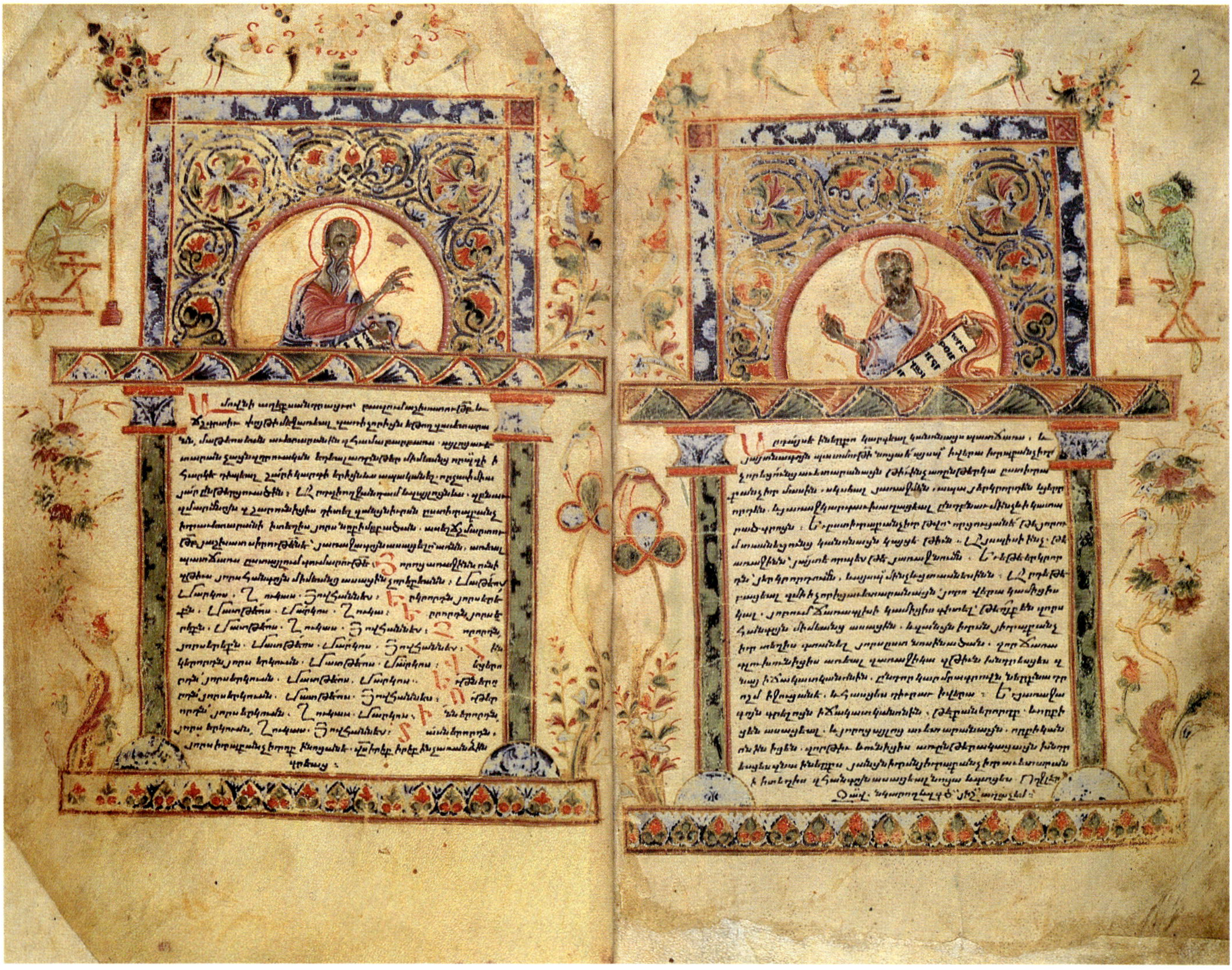

Fols.1b–2a. The Letter of Eusebius to Carpianus
The inscription reads: 'Zavag nkarol ew zgc[ol] yiš[ea] alač em'.

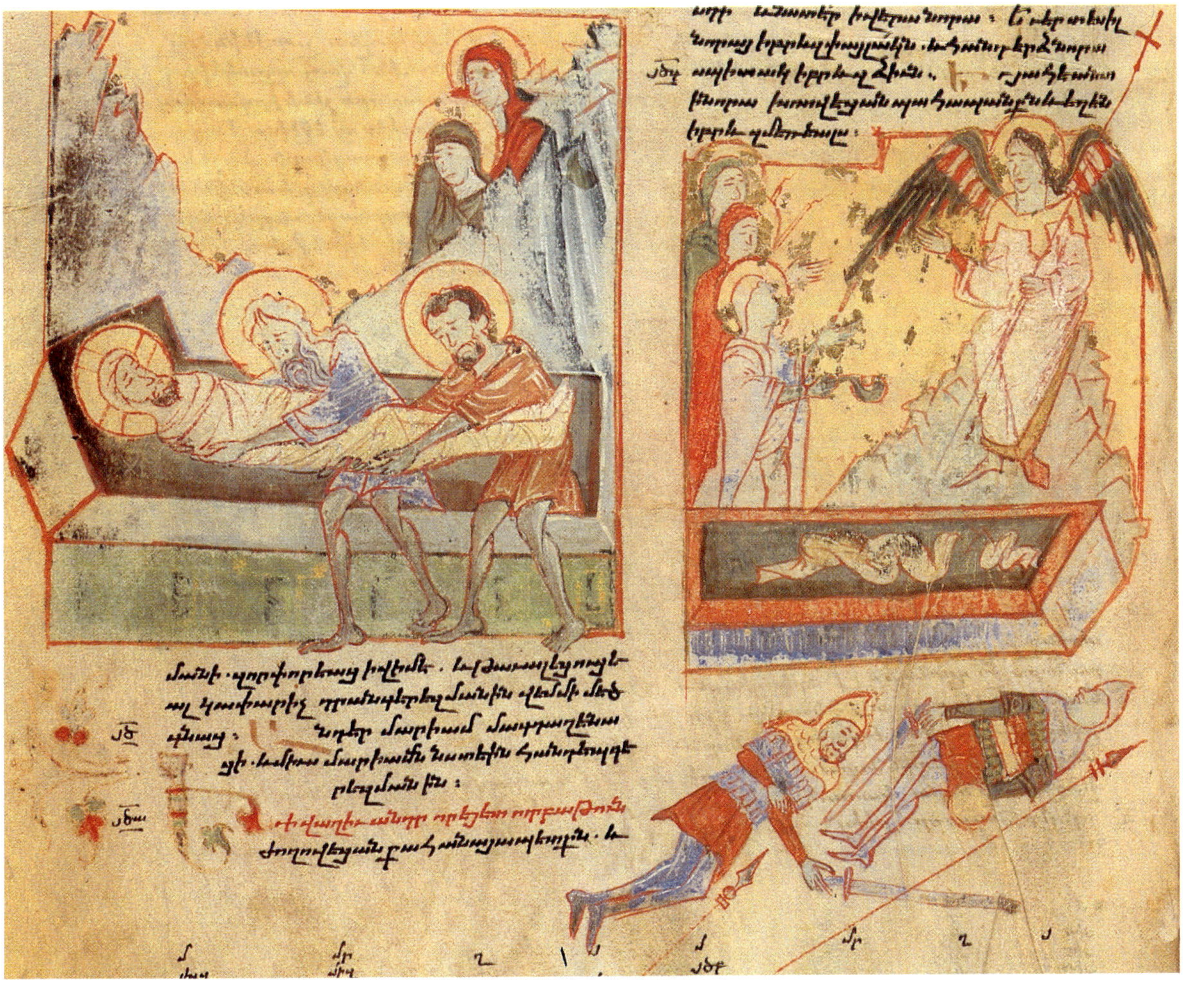

Fol.23b. The Entombment and The Holy Women at the Sepulchre
Two aged men, in short tunics, Joseph and Nicodemus, walk one behind the other, carry the shrouded body of Christ and 'laid it in a clean new tomb'; behind the men stand 'Mary Magdalene and the other Mary'. In the background rugged mountains (St Matthew 27:57–61).

The three women Mary Magdalene, and Mary the mother of James, and Salome (Mark 16:1) *carrying spices to anoint Him, approach the angel who is seated on the rock holding a cross in one hand, and with the other hand points to the sepulchre which is empty, except the 'linen cloth lying there rolled up'* (John 20:6–7). *In the foreground two soldiers prostrate, asleep; their swords and lances lie on the ground next to them* (Matthew 28:1–6).

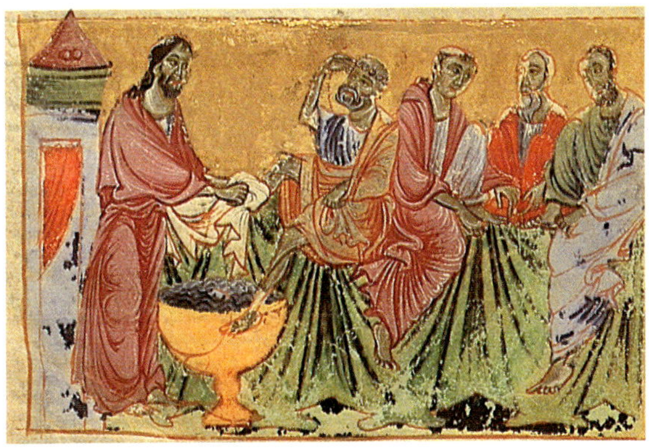

Fol.65a. Washing of the Feet
Christ, standing inside a doorway, wipes the right foot of Peter, with a white towel, who is seated on a high stool and points to his head. Three other apostles in a group sit behind him. The apostles are without nimbs. As in many Armenian manuscripts, the Washing of the Feet rather than the Last Supper is selected to represent the Passion Week.

FOUR GOSPELS (MS Or.2680)

Manuscript on paper, 251 folios, excluding two vellum fly-leaves, in twenty-two quires of twelve leaves each measuring 24 × 32 cm. Text in *bolorgir* written in two columns of twenty-one lines each.

PROVENANCE The manuscript was copied by the scribe Astuacatur, in 1317 (fols. 77b, 194a), for the monk Atom, who deposited it at the church of Holy Astuacacin at Kar̄bi. The last owner of the manuscript, archdeacon Sargis and his brother Alekʿsanos, renewed and rebound the manuscript in 1563 and presented it to the church of St Sargis.

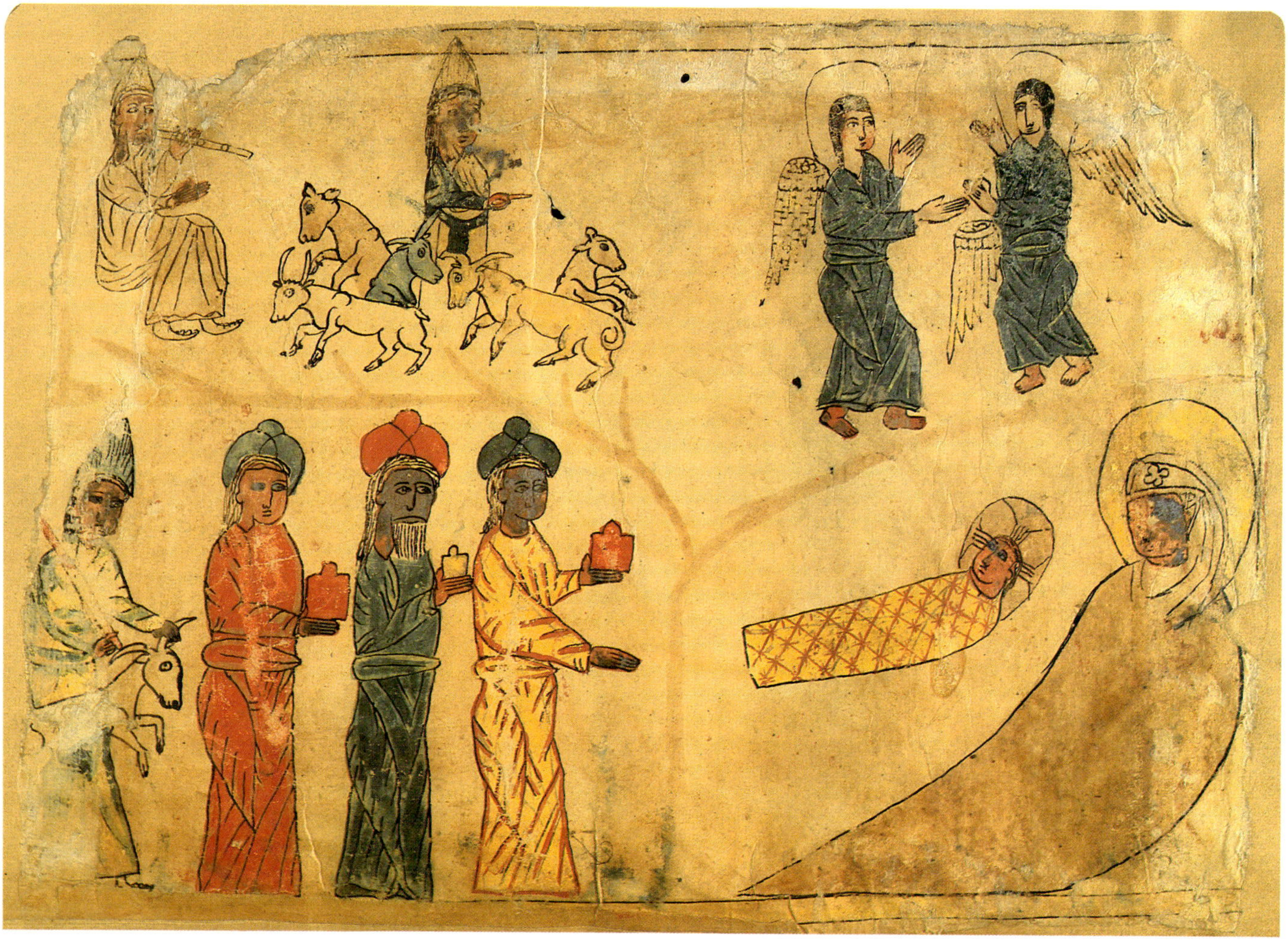

Fol.2b. The Nativity and the adoration of the Magi
At the top left is a shepherd seated, playing a flute, and another standing, both with peaked helmet-type caps, and a group of five sheep. At the bottom left, the three Magi approach in long robes and turbans, bearing gifts. Behind them, extreme left is a shepherd with crook and sheep. At the top right are two angels in blue robes with wings and haloes. At the mid lower right is the Christ child, in swaddling clothes, his head to the right, with halo and below him the Virgin Mary, reclining to the right, in a long robe shown in outline only, with head-dress and a yellow halo.

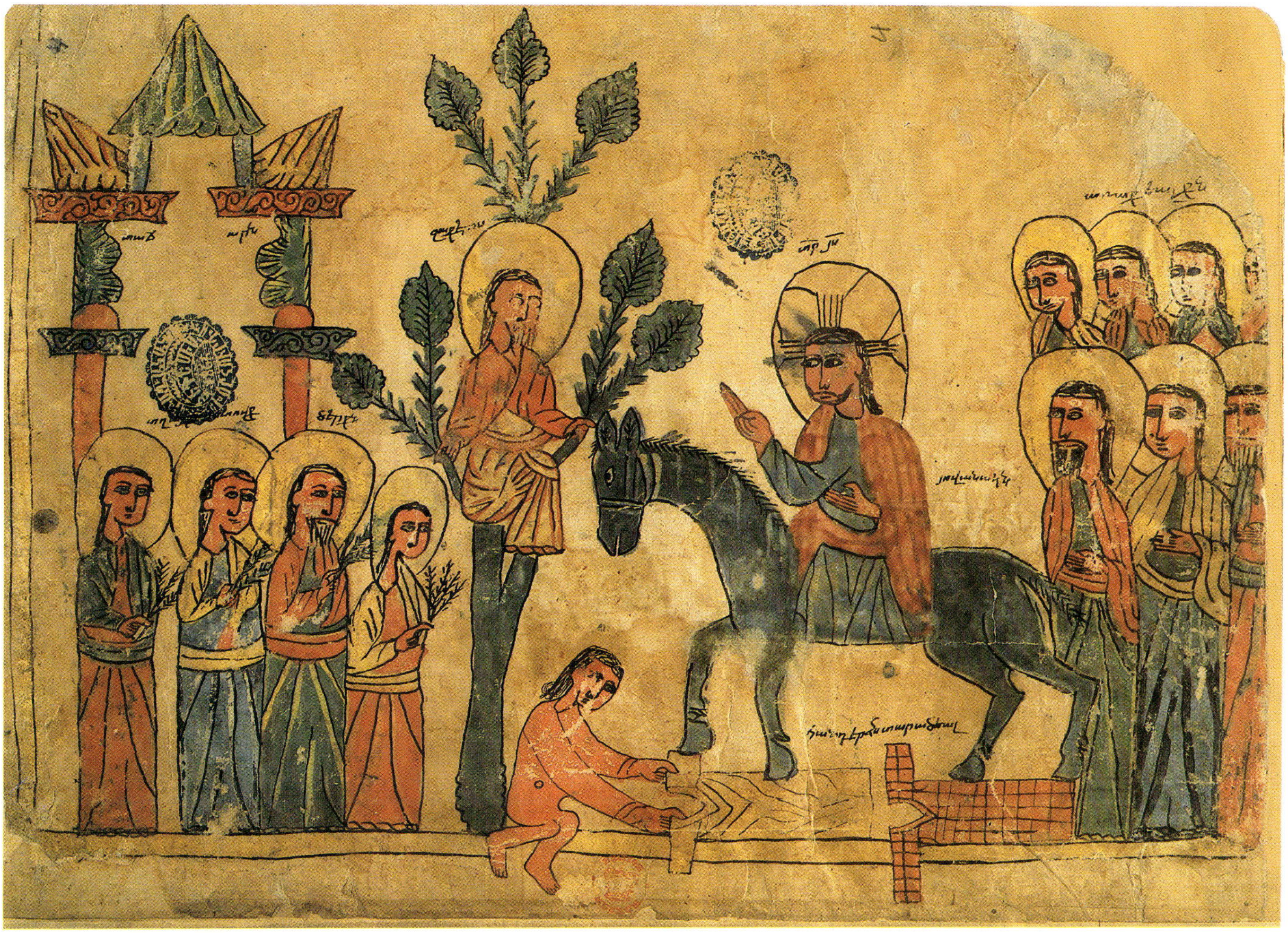

Fol.4a. Christ's Entry into Jerusalem

The top left has a gateway with three triangular elements above representing the 'temple' as in the Presentation in the Temple (fol. 3a left). At the bottom left are four disciples with haloes and with palm branches in their hands, facing right. In the centre is a tall tree with a few elaborately represented branches, with Zaccheus sitting amid the branches. At the centre left Christ on the donkey moves from right to left. A small figure facing right kneels before the donkey's feet, where two shirts are spread in the way, one yellow and one red. Christ is clad in red over blue, with black hair and short beard, with halo. He rides with his right hand outstretched in blessing. Behind him, to the right, are two ranks of four and three disciples with haloes, wearing long robes.

FOUR GOSPELS (MS Or.2707)

Manuscript on paper, 295 folios, in twenty-six quires of ten leaves each, except the last, which has eight leaves. Size 13·5 × 8·5 cm. Text is fairly clear *bolorgir* in two columns of twenty-three lines each.

PROVENANCE Gospel-book copied in AD 1542 'in the land of Bžuniq, now called Xlatʿ (Ahlat), in the village called Šołacʿ by the hand of the sinful Karapet, from a choice and accurate model', during the patriarchate of Grigor XI Biwzandacʿi (1536–1545) and the reign of Sultan Sulaymān (1520–1566).

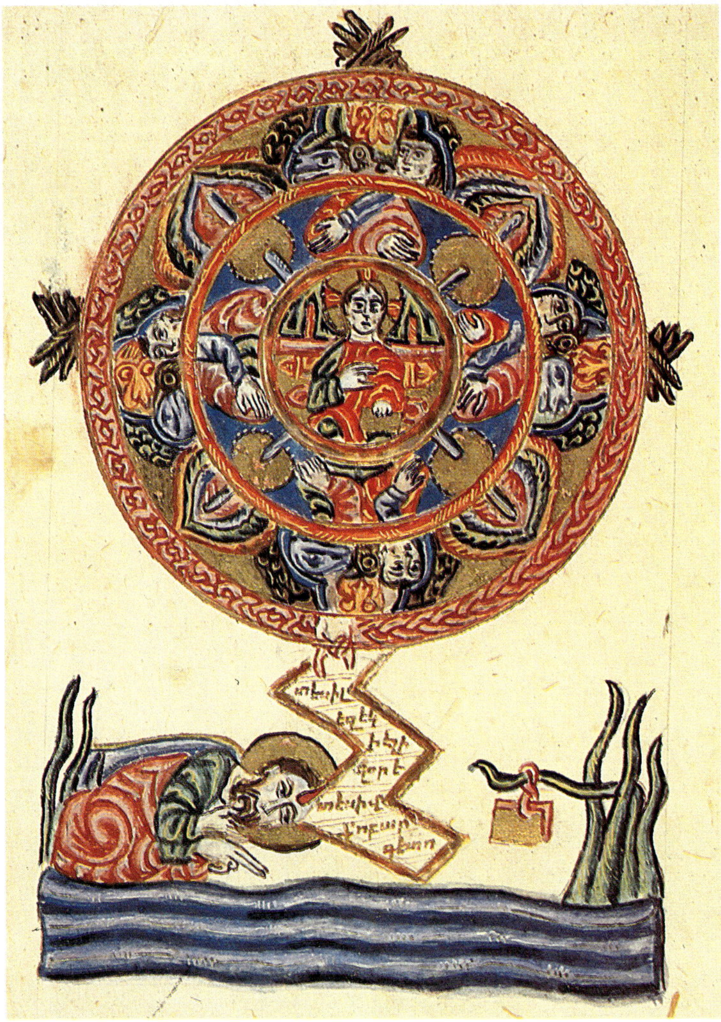

Fol.7b. The Vision of Ezekiel

Ezekiel kneels, by the bank of the river Qobar, below a large central medallion with the figure of a beardless Christ enthroned in the inner-most part of the three concentric circles which represent 'the wheel within the wheel'; the wheels, shaped like gold discs, are shown in the second circle; the apocalyptic 'creatures' occupy this zone and the third, with the circle passing through their bodies at the neck. The tetramorphs are drawn in the diagonal axes, their bodies cut by the second circle and their wings projecting beyond the outer circle. A blessing hand extending from below the medallion holds a scroll on which the title of the scene is inscribed, while a closed book is dangling from one of the reeds (Revelation 10:9–11).

Fol.8b. The Tree of Jesse

The artists of Cilicia represented the Tree of Jesse in a marginal composition on the opening page of the Gospel of Matthew, next to the genealogy of Christ. It is only in the fifteenth century that this typological scene becomes part of the Gospel cycle in manuscripts illustrated in the area of Lake Van. The Tree of Jesse in our manuscript differs both from the composition represented by T'oros of Taron and from the marginal miniatures in Cilician manuscripts. The tree, coming out of Jesse's side, separates at the top into two large palm leaves which frame the bust figures of the Virgin and Child; the twenty-eight ancestors, bust figures of nimbed men and women holding scrolls are painted one above the other next to the trunk of the tree, in rows of two and three, separated by palm leaves.

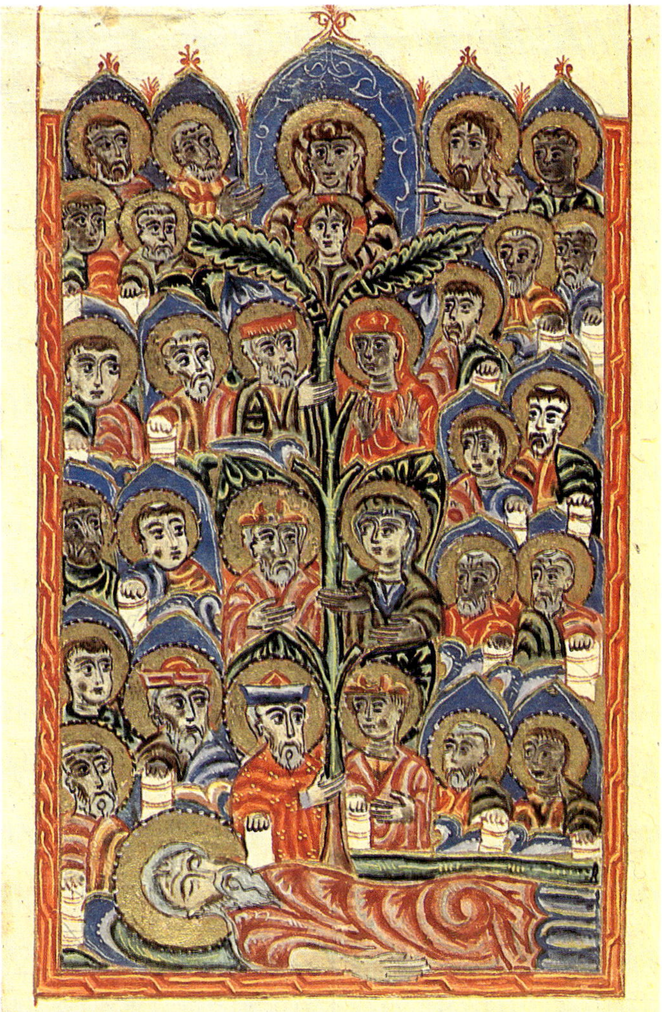

FOUR GOSPELS (MS Or.5737)

Manuscript on paper, 309 folios, in twenty-four quires of twelve leaves; the first twenty-six folios are not included in these quires. Size 17 × 13·5 cm. Written in large, elegant *bolorgir* in two columns of twenty-one lines each.

PROVENANCE This manuscript was copied by the priest Step῾annos in AD 1608 in the city of Šoš 'which is translated Aspahan' [i.e. Isfahān] for the sponsors *khwāja* Vēlijan and his wife Gayianē. In the same year the artist Mesrop, son of Martiros of Khizan (see MS Or.2707) 'illuminated the book with lovely colours, gold and *lapis lazuli*, and all sorts of pigments' during the catholicate of Tēr Melik῾set and Dawit IV Vałaršapatec῾i (1590–1629) and the reign of 'the wise Shah 'Abbas the red headed' (fols. 303, 304b). The artist has signed his name under the portrait of the Holy Virgin (fol. 16b) and a Canon table (fol. 27a) as 'Mesropik całkoł'.

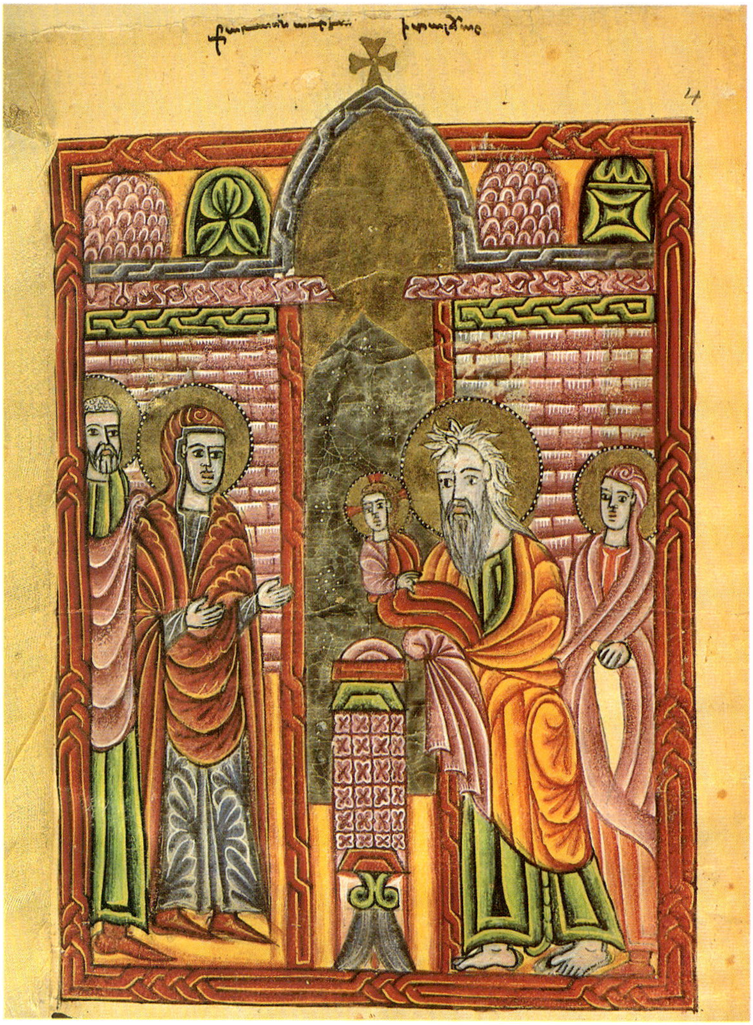

Fol.4a. The Presentation of Christ in the Temple
The Virgin and Joseph, without doves, Simēon with the Christ Child in his arms, and the prophetess Anna, holding an open scroll.

Fol.15a. The Last Judgement

Christ is enthroned on the four symbolic beasts all with wings, His feet resting on a richly decorated semi-circular cushion; Christ is holding a book in one hand resting on His knees and with the other hand is blessing. The Virgin and John the Baptist stand at His sides in the attitude of prayer. The scales hang from the centre of the lower frame, the left tray rests on the back of a demon, a second demon tries to pull down the right tray, a third demon with a load on his back stands behind him. An angel, standing on the left, pierces the demons with a lance. Inscription: 'The judgement'.

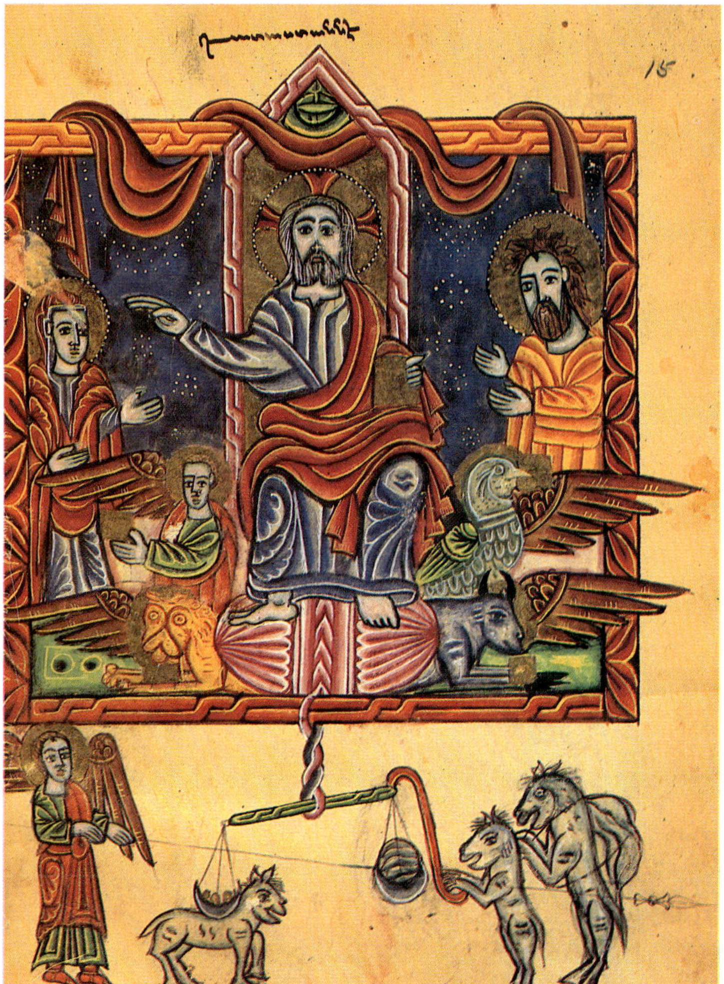

FOUR GOSPELS (MS Or.5449)

Manuscript on fine vellum, 271 folios, in twenty-one quires, mostly of twelve leaves each. Size 13·7 × 10 cm. Text in *bolorgir* written in two columns of twenty-three lines each.

PROVENANCE The manuscript was written in AD 1683 for the sponsors *Paron* Ałavēlin, and his partner in life, Xanpʻar Xačʻik. The calligraphy and style of illumination are closely related to those favoured by the Armenian *atélier* in Isfahān of the seventeenth century.

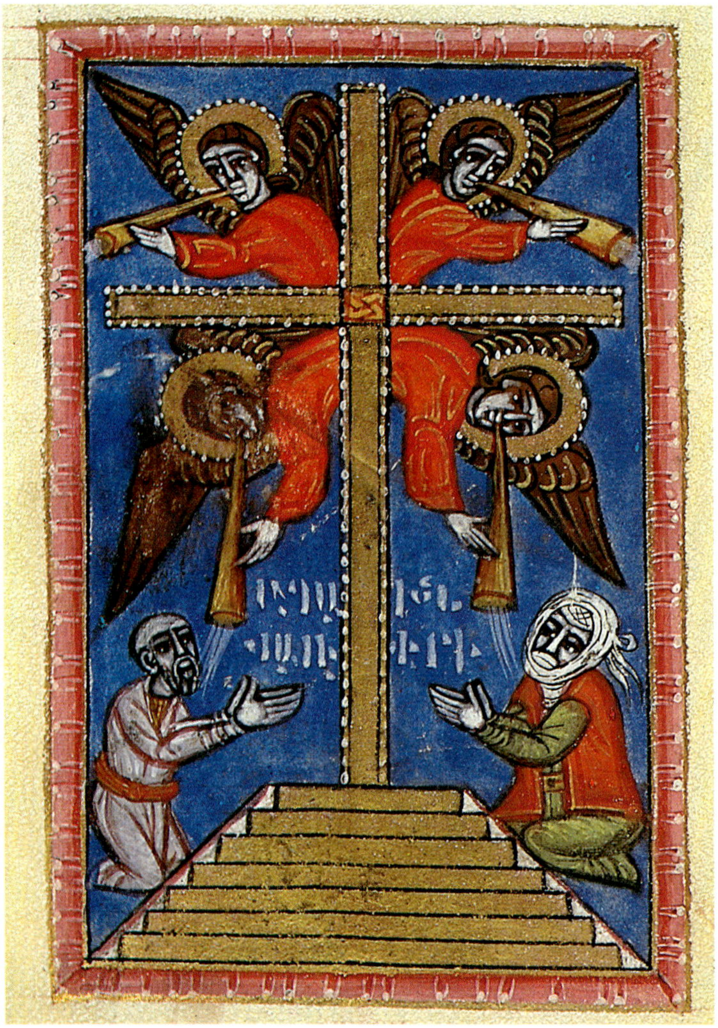

Fol.15b. Christ in Glory

This composition is based on the text of Matthew 24:30-31. In one of the Armenian prayers recited during the octave of the feast of the Exaltation of the Cross, the cross is identified with Christ: 'O holy Cross, when thou shalt shine in the East, in an ineffable light, and shalt illuminate the faithful and condemn the infidel race of the Jews, illuminate me also'.

An ornate cross, 'the sign of the Son of man', is raised on a seven stepped pedestal; in each angle made by the cross there is an angel trumpeting. The donors of the manuscript are kneeling to the left and right at the foot of the cross. The Armenian inscription on the blue background gives the names of the donors: 'Ałavali [and] X[a]npʻ[a] ri'.

FOUR GOSPELS (MS Or.14161)

Manuscript on vellum, 301 folios plus two fly-leaves, in gatherings of twelve leaves. Size 8 × 5 cm. Written in a small regular *bolorgir* in double columns of twenty-four lines each.

PROVENANCE According to the colophon (fols. 302–302b) the manuscript was copied by the scribe Xač'atur *dpir* [clerk], and completed on Thursday, 2 January AD 1695, at the Church of St George the General called *Sulu Manastir* [the 'Watery Monastery', near Samatya Kapisi on the Marmara shore] in Constantinople. The artist is named in the colophon as the worthless Gabriēl who in 1694 painted at the same church of St George the Gospel-book MS 319 now in the Mekhitharist Library in Vienna.

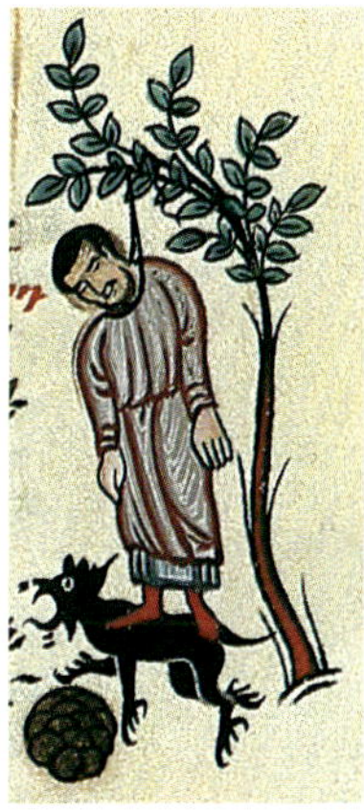

Fol.98a. Judas hanging from a tree, with the demon and the coins strewed at the foot of the demon (St Matthew 27:5–6)

Fol.8a. The Last Supper

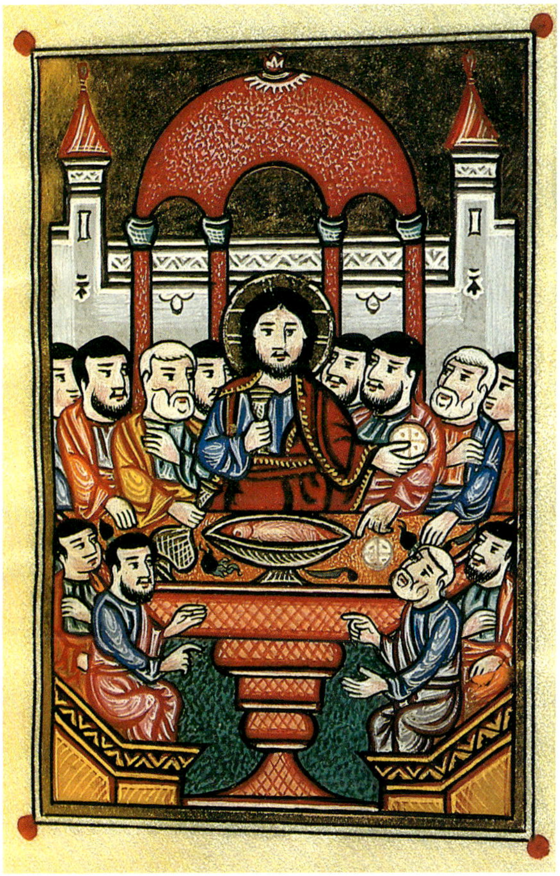

Fol.9b. The Washing of the feet

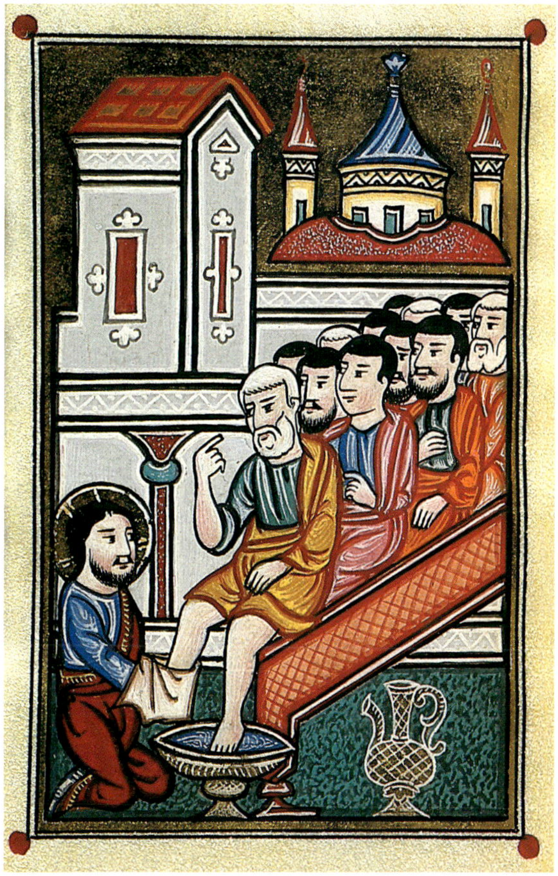

PLATE XIX

Four Gospels (MS Or.13895)

Manuscript on vellum, 333 folios, in twenty-six quires of twelve leaves. Size 19 × 14 cm. Text written in regular *bolorgir* in two columns of twenty-two lines to the page.

PROVENANCE The colophon (fols. 329b–330b) records that the manuscript was copied and illuminated by Nikołayos, pupil of Tēr Zakʻaria, and completed on 20 May 1107 (30 May 1658) during the catholicate of Yakob IV of New Julfa (1655–80) and the episcopate 'of the northern regions' (Crimea) of Grigor 'who died in this year'. The Gospel was commissioned by *khwāja* Kirakos, son of the pilgrim (*mahdesi*) Dōlvadiar, as a memorial for his deceased relatives.

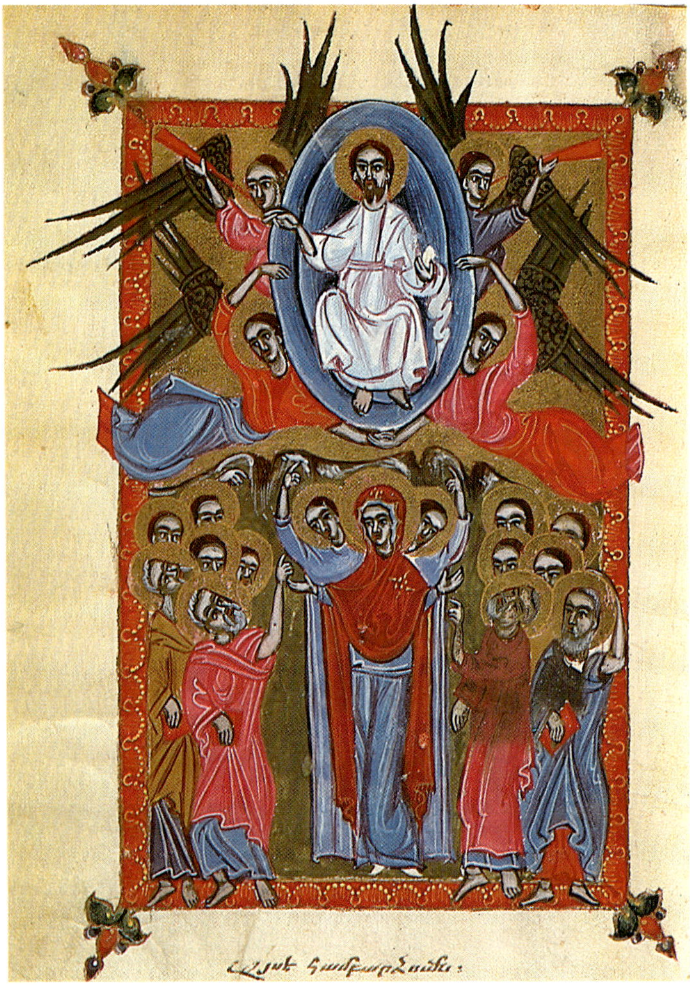

Fol.12b. The Ascension
Christ is seated in an oval mandorla borne by four angels two of whom have trumpets. Below are the Virgin in the centre with the group of six apostles on either side gazing upwards. The inscription reads: 'The Ascension'.

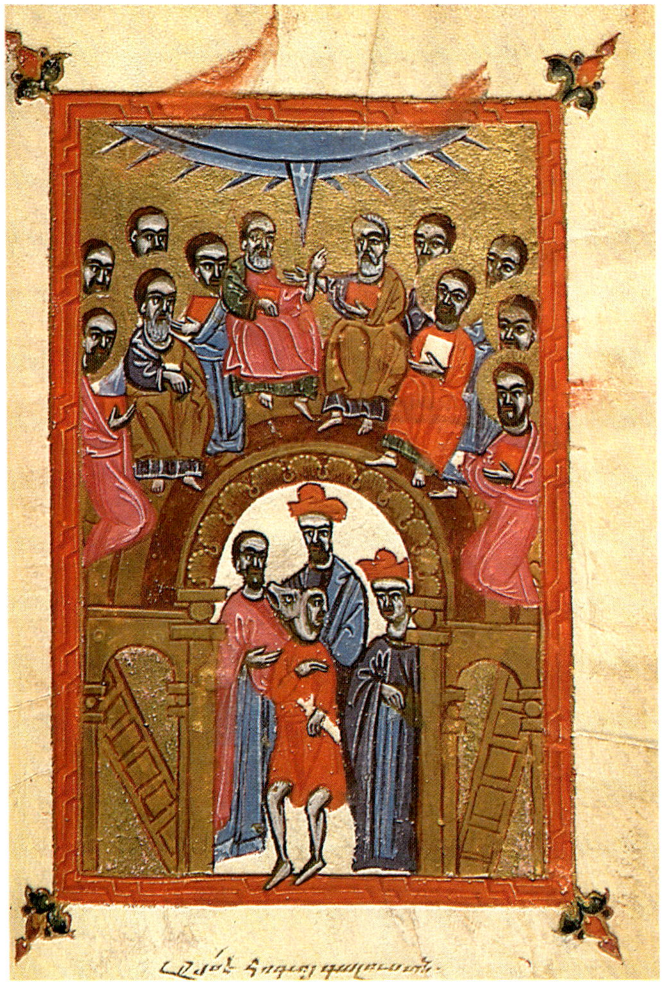

Fol.13a. Pentecost
The apostles are seated, in groups of six in the high chamber. Under the arc inside the gate opening into the upper chamber, flanked by two staircases stand three figures, two wearing red turbans and a semi-naked figure which appears to be a demoniac, has a human head, from the right of which protrudes an animal head. This figure represents one of the pagan peoples from the distant land. The inscription reads: 'This is the coming of the spirit'.

FOUR GOSPELS (MS Or.2668)

Manuscript on oriental paper, 344 folios, excluding two vellum folios bound at each end, in twenty-eight quires of twelve leaves. The preliminary illuminated folios are not included in the quires. Text in large, regular *bolorgir*, written in double columns of twenty lines each. Size 20 × 10·5 cm.

PROVENANCE This Gospel-book was written in AD 1437 at the Monastery of St George in the province of Balu 'during the bitter and cruel time, when untimely death at the hands of unbelievers, made impossible for priests to eat bread', when Hamzah Sultan was governor of Mesopotamia, and Constantine VI of Vahkay was Catholicos of Cilician Armenia (1429–1439). The manuscript was copied and illuminated by the priest Awetikʿ for the sponsors Ahli Melikʿ, daughter of Tawlatʿ Melikʿ 'who acquired this holy Gospel out of her fair and honest earnings as a memorial and intercessor with God for herself and her parents' (fol. 340b).

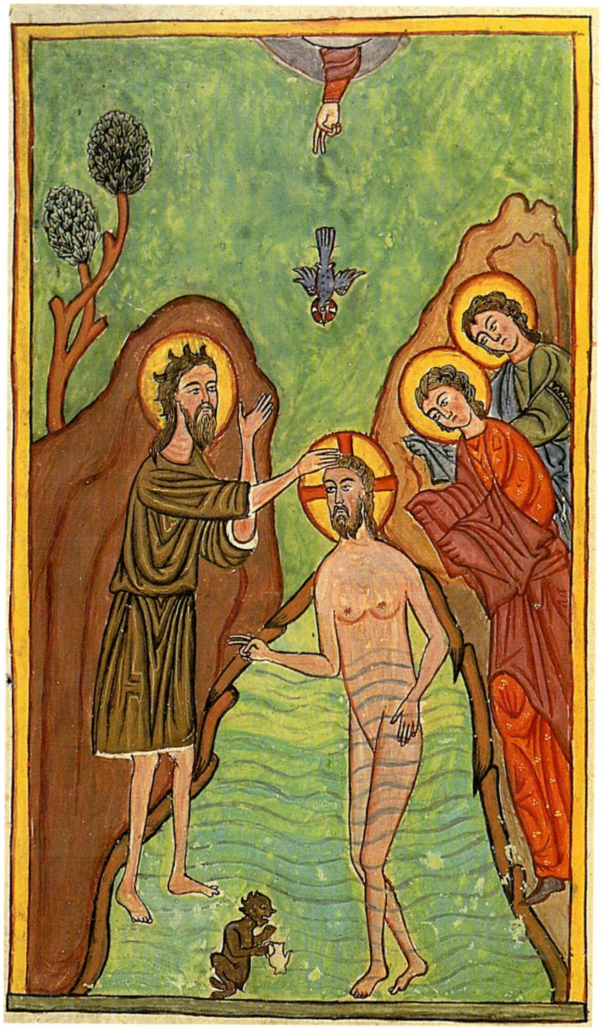

Fol.2b. The Baptism of Christ
John the Baptist, wearing a brown smock, stands in the water, lays his right hand on the head of Christ, who stands full face, naked in a horizontal band of water which comes up to his waist line. Below John's feet is a small devil with a pitcher. To the right, two haloed figures attend, bending over towards Christ. The allegorical figure of the Jordan who flees, overturning his pitcher, is a literal interpretation of the words of the psalmist, 'The sea saw it and fled; Jordan was driven back', words which all the gospel commentators have related to the Baptism. At the top centre is a segment of sky, with the hand of God pointing down to the dove of the Holy Spirit, descending on Christ. The faces are effectively and movingly drawn.

Fol.3b. The Transfiguration of Christ.

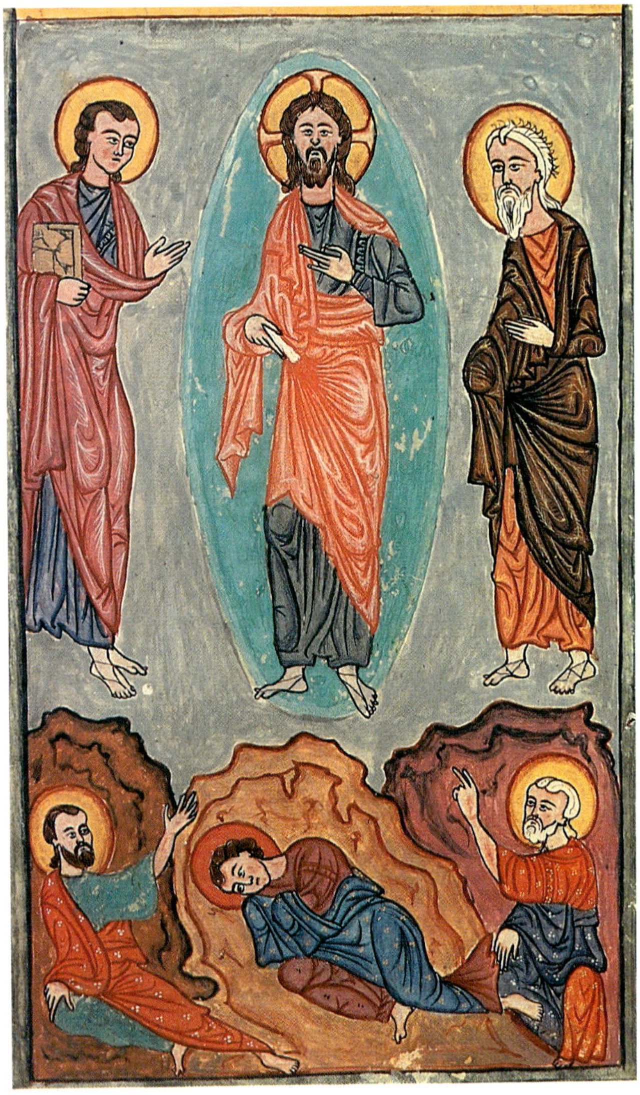

Fol.5b. The Entombment of Christ
At the centre, Christ's body lies with head to the left and turned away; he is wrapped in white grave clothes, and his nimbus shows behind his head. Joseph of Arimathea, and Nicodemus at the head and the foot grasp Christ's body. To the left and right behind each man stands a weeping woman. Above is a purple background of the night; below there are bands of brown and grey wash.

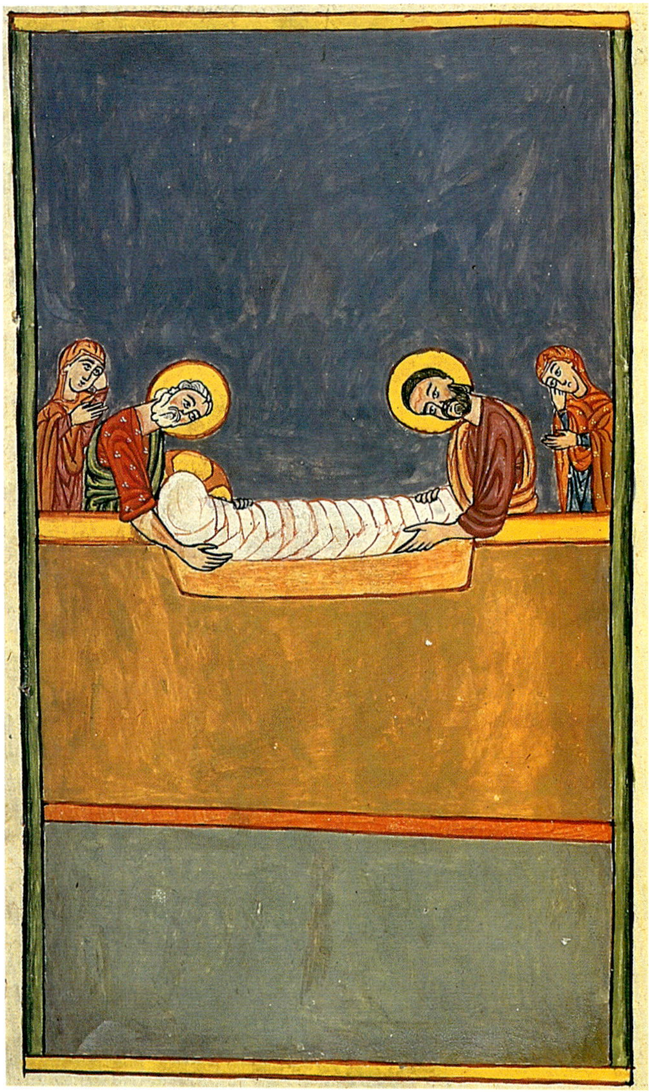

Four Gospels (Add. MS 7940)

Manuscript on oriental paper, 349 folios, in twenty-six quires, mostly of twelve leaves. Text in neat *bolorgir* written in double columns of twenty-two lines between lines vertically ruled of red and green. Size 8·5 × 5 cm.

PROVENANCE There is no scribal colophon. Two columns of inscriptions, on fol. 346b, have been carefully effaced. On fol. 347, in a small current hand, Avet Setʿean notes that Petros Setʿean gave the manuscript to the priest Petros in sign of friendship. On fols. 1, 3, 7, 26b are the stamps of seal bearing the words 'servant of Jesus, Melikʿ Simēōn, 1224' (AD 1774). The date of the manuscript is of about AD 1600.

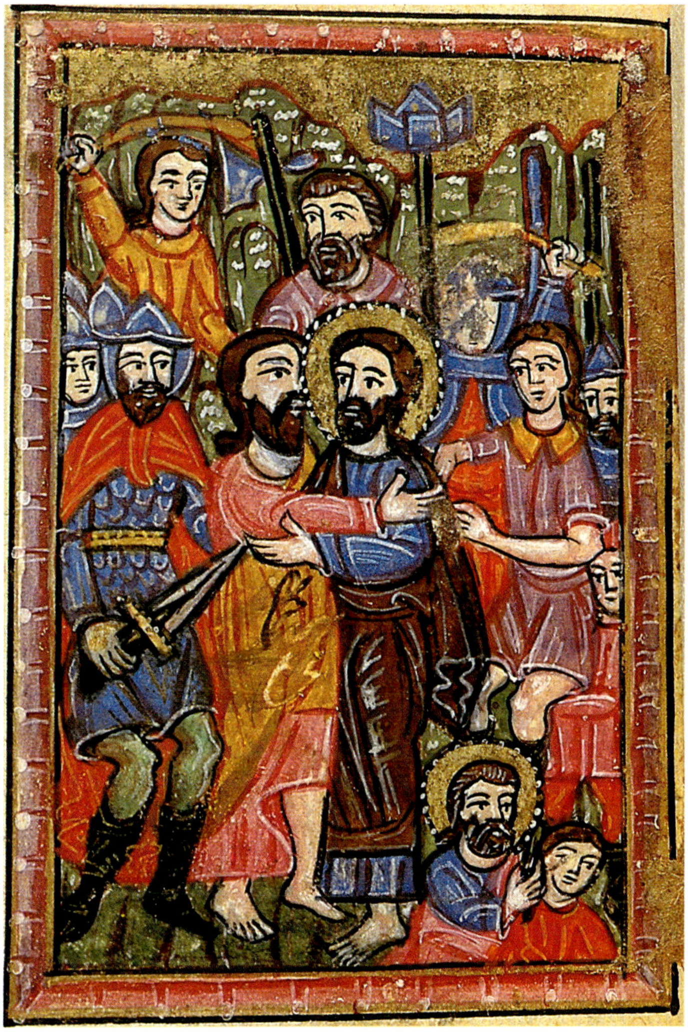

Fol.9b. Betrayal
Judas, coming from the left, embraces Christ; helmeted soldiers carrying lances and torches surround them. In the lower right corner Peter, kneeling, raises his sword over Malchus, who lies on the floor and is depicted like a small child.

Four Gospels (MS Or.5761)

Manuscript on fine vellum, (fols. 20–149) and oriental paper (fols. 1–19 and 150–254). The vellum sheets are palimpsest of a Latin manuscript in Gothic hand, probably a law book, the rubrics of which are still discernible. Text in large *bolorgir* of the sixteenth century, in double columns of twenty-three lines each. Size 15·5 × 10·5 cm.

PROVENANCE This manuscript was illustrated by Yovhannēs, son of Zakʿaria and Ełisē in AD 1402, in the city of Muš in Tarōn. The artist has left his signature at the end of the Letter of Eusebius to Carpianus (fol. 2a). The manuscript was commissioned by Łazar, as a memorial for himself and his parents, when 'the catholicos of the Armenians was Tēr Karapet [I Kełecʿi, 1393–1404]'.

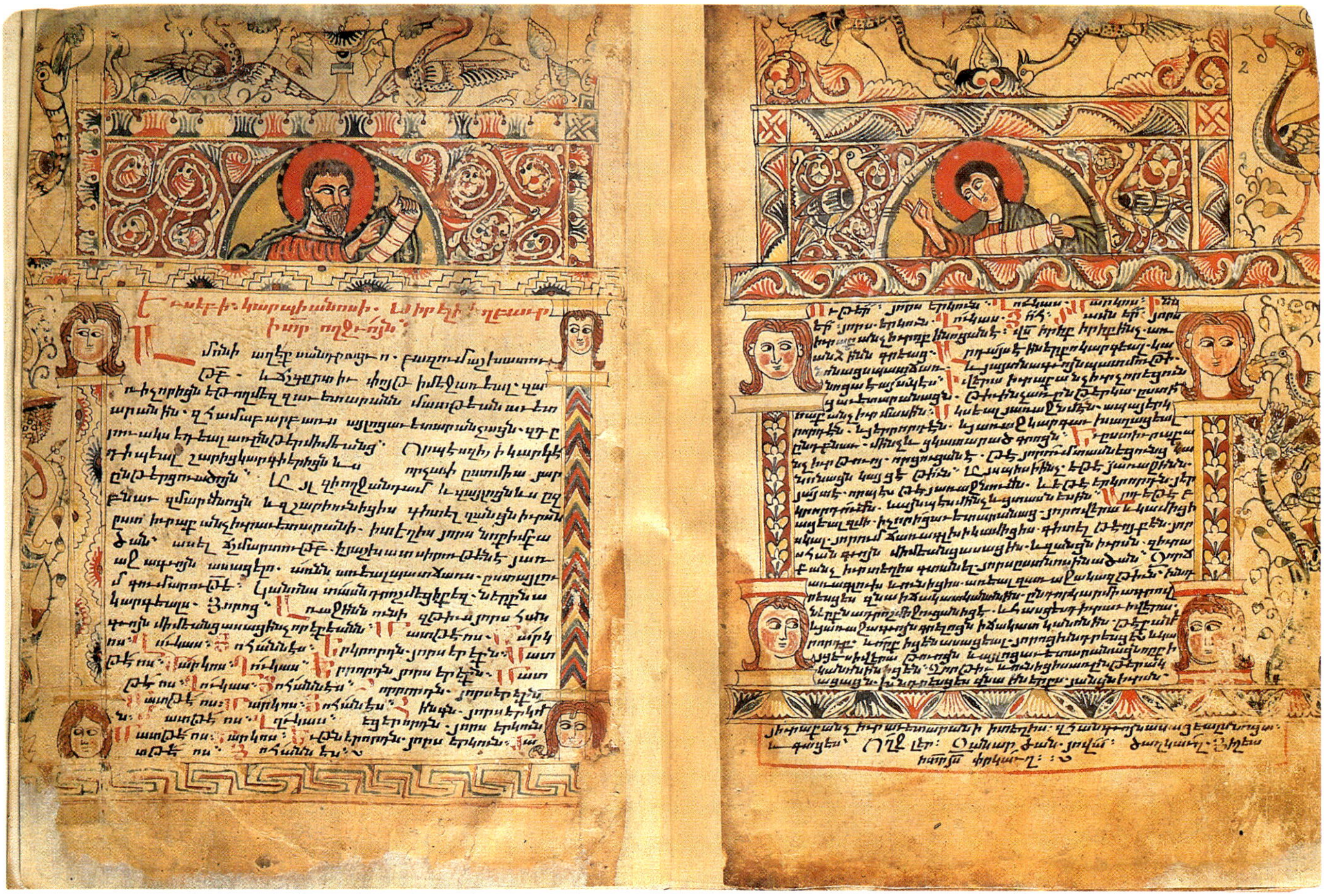

Fols.1b–2a. Letter of Eusebius to Carpianus

PLATE XXIV

Fol.9a. Headpiece of St Matthew's Gospel
The headpiece of the Gospel is decorated with the figures of the Virgin and Child and two angels placed above the frame. A large ornament of interlacing palmettes fills the outer margin. The initial letter 'G' is a historiated capital: a young angel holding a book: followed by two lines of festooned letters, followed by lines of red uncials.

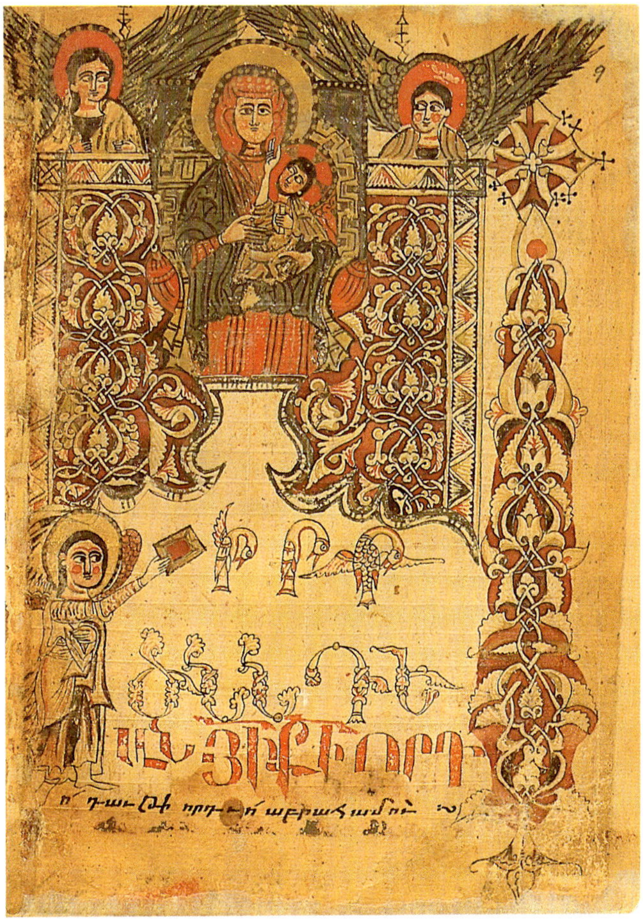

APPENDICES

APPENDIX A

Armenian Gospel Books in the British Library in Chronological Sequence

MS NO	*Conybeare Catalogue No*	*Physical Description*	*Script*	*Date*	*Place*
Add.21932	1, pp. 1–2	Vellum; 244 fols.	*erkatʻagir*	Tenth cent.	unknown
Add.19727	2, pp. 2–4	Glazed Eastern paper; 310 fols.	square *erkatʻagir*	1166	unknown
Or.81	4, pp. 4–6	Vellum; 375 fols.	*erkatʻagir*	1181	Drazark
Or.13654	See *BLJ*, III, 2 (1977), 139–66	Vellum; 384 fols.	upright *erkatʻagir*	1200–02	Awag Vankʻ
Or.2678	5, pp. 6–7	Glazed paper; 290 fols.	irregular *bolorgir*	1207	Cilicia
Add.18549	8, pp. 11–14	Fine Vellum; 314 fols.	medium *bolorgir*	1280	Sis
Or.5626	11, pp. 17–18	Vellum; 344 fols.	elegant *bolorgir*	1282	Drazark
Or.2283	10, pp. 15–17	Oriental paper; 295 fols.	*bolorgir*	1295	convent of Tʻełenikʻ
Or.10960	—	Glazed paper; 202 fols.	elegant *bolorgir*	1295	Gṙner ?
Add.27489	12, pp. 18–19	Vellum; 203 fols.	large *bolorgir*	13–14th cent.	Cilicia
Or.2679	6, pp. 7–9	Glazed paper; 292 fols.	regular *bolorgir*	1281	canton of Arčeš, monastery of Yaspisênkal

Scribe	*Artist*	*Illuminations and Illustrations*	*Remarks*
unknown	unknown	None	This MS omits Mark XVI: vv. 9–20.
Simēon	—	Headpieces (fols. 8, 92, 147, 240); Canon Tables (fols. 4–7); Letter of Eusebius (fol. 3b).	The scribe has used the era of Yovhannēs *sarkawag* which began in 1084 and of which the 82 year would be AD 1166. Second colophon is dated 1440.
Tʿorōs	Xačʿatur	Five portraits (fols. 1b, 8b, 111b, 180b, 289b); Headpieces (fols. 9, 112, 181, 290); Letter of Eusebius (fols. 2b–3a); Canon Tables (fols. 4b–7a).	Bought of Joseph Lilly, 22 April, 1868.
Vardan *dpir*	—	Letter of Eusebius (fols. 1b, 2a); Canon Tables (fols. 3b, 4a, 5b, 6a); Headpieces (fols. 7a, 117a, 182a, 299a).	The memorialist Grigor Daranałcʿi (1576–1643) gives the account of the forced deportation of Armenians from Anatolia in 1605, when the MS was brought to Constantinople by the refugees from Kemakh.
Grigor ?	—	No decorations. Gospels begin with ornate capitals (fols. 79b, 131b, 223a); rectangular designs for numbers of the lections.	Belonged to the Armenian Prelacy of Edessa 1868; bought of S. Baronian, 9 Nov. 1883.
Stepʿanos Vahkaycʿi		Portraits of the Evangelists (fols. 3b, 43b, 70b, 112b), Peter & Paul (fol. 161b); Headpieces (fols. 4a, 44a, 71a, 113, 162, 253); 23 figures of saints in the margins of Acts & Catholic Epistles; oblong frontispiece for the rest of the books.	In 1618 the MS was in the possession of *xawjay* Nazar in Julfa, who had it repaired and illuminated by the artist Mesrop Xizancʿi. The pictures of the Saints and the portraits were added in the seventeenth century.
Barseł	Yoh[anēs]	Portraits of the Evangelists (fols. 1b, 101b, 161b, 266b); Headpieces (fols. 2, 102, 162, 267).	In the year 1426 the manuscript was in the possession of Martiros, who presented it to the church of Holy Astuacacin at Sanahin, where it was restored by Yoh[anēs] '*spasawor surb Astuacacni*'. This Yoh[anēs] is the artist of St Matthew's portrait and headpiece & St Mark's headpiece. The portraits of Luke and John belong to another artist and St Mark's to a third.
Kʿahanay, Šmawon and David	—	Headpieces (fols. 4, 93, 145, 227).	The copying of the MS was begun by the brothers Kʿahanay and Šmawon, and was completed by David after the death of Kʿahanay.
Tʿoros Vahkaycʿi	—	Headpieces (fols. 1, 43, 70, 114, 142); marginal miniatures: Matthew (3), Mark (4), Luke (8), and John (4).	Contains the Four Gospels & The Vision of the prophet Isaiah. The MS is the first half of Add. MS19730 (Conybeare, pp. 9–11).
unknown	—	Letter of Eusebius (fols. 3b–4a); Canon Tables (fols. 5b–12a); Headpieces (fols. 14, 77, 118); picture of the Crucifixion in the margin of fol. 69b.	The writing as far as fol. 141 is in clear *bolorgir* but from fol. 142 another hand continues in a less archaic style.
unknown	—	Arcades for the Letter of Eusebius (fols. 1b–2a); Headpiece, with portraits of Matthew and John (fols. 5b, 222b); Full-figure of the Virgin Mary (fol. 81b) precedes Mark's Gospel; Portrait of Luke standing in the margin (fol. 131b) whose Gospel begins on fol. 132a. Small headpiece and long ornate initial for each Gospel (fols. 6, 82, 132, 223).	The MS has a second colophon (fol. 291) written in 1346, when the illustrations were added. Later in 1553 the MS was given to the church of Astuacacin in Uṙhay. Imprint of an Armenian seal (fols. 5b, 81b, 111a) record that the MS belonged to 'the prelacy of the Armenian church in Edessa, 1868'. Bought of S. Baronian, 9 Nov. 1883.

APPENDIX A

MS NO	*Conybeare Catalogue No*	*Physical Description*	*Script*	*Date*	*Place*
Or.2680	13, pp. 20–22	Glazed paper; 251 fols.	*bolorgir*	1317	Vawṙay/Kaṙboy
Add.15411	14, pp. 22–24	Vellum; 312 fols.	*bolorgir*	1321	Gladjor monastery
Or.5304	16, pp. 27–28	Fine vellum; 75 fols.	neat *bolorgir*	1329–58	Sultaniya
Or.5761	21, pp. 36–39	Vellum/paper; 254 fols.	*bolorgir*	1402	Tarōn
Or.2668	18, pp. 29–32	Oriental paper; 344 fols.	*bolorgir*	1437	Balu at the Surb Gēorg vankʿ
Or.2681	15, pp. 24–27	Oriental paper; 293 fols.	*bolorgir*	1484	Jerusalem
Or.82	17, pp. 28–29	Fine vellum; 294 fols.	*bolorgir*	15th cent.	Amida ?
Or.2707	19, pp. 32–35	Oriental paper; 295 fols.	*bolorgir*	1541	Bžunik, now called X
Or.13933	—	Paper; 261 fols.	*bolorgir*	1575	—

Scribe	*Artist*	*Illuminations and Illustrations*	*Remarks*
Astuacatur	—	Canon Tables (fols. 1, 7–9b); Cycle of Gospel scenes (fols. 2b–5b); Letter of Eusebius (fols. 6a/b); Headpieces (fols. 10, 78, 122, 195); Portraits (fols. 121b, 194b).	In 1563 the manuscript was repaired and presented to the church of Saint Sargis. On fols. 7, 76, 195 there is a blue stamp bearing the words 'T'ałakan xorhurd Yedesia, 1868'. This MS was bought of S. Baronian, 9 Nov. 1883.
Kiwron	T'oros Tarōnac'i	Canon Tables (fols. 1–8); Portraits (fols. 9b, 91b, 241b); Headpieces (fols. 10, 92, 148, 242); Marginal miniatures: Matthew (9), Mark (7), Luke (12), and John (13).	The last owner of the MS, Safar *xawjay*, had the manuscript repaired in 1621 in Isfahan. This Safar is not the brother of *xawjay* Nazar who had died in 1618. This Safar who wrote in 1621 names his father as being Tēr Petros and his mother as sult'an Xat'un. *Cf.* Add. MS 18549.
Awag	—	Letter of Eusebius (fols. 1b–2a); Canon Tables (fols. 3b–8a); Portraits (fols. 25b, 36b, 56b); Headpieces (fols. 9a, 26a, 37a, 57a, 70b); Marginal miniatures (*see* Appendix B).	Conybeare assigns the MS to the years 1400 to 1500. The name of the scribe which allows us to date the MS is written at the end of the Letter of Eusebius: 'I beseech you to remember Awag the painter and scribe'.
Yovhannēs	—	Letter of Eusebius (fols. 1b–2a); Canon Tables (fols. 2b–6a); Portraits (fols. 8b, 82b, 134b, 206b); Headpieces (fols. 9, 83, 135, 207); *The Last Judgment* (fol. 1a).	The vellum folios are palimpsest of a Latin MS in Gothic hand. Later colophons of owners are dated 1568, 1581, and 1611. The illuminator of the paper portions added the illuminations in the vellum portions. A later hand has drawn the picture of the Last Judgement.
Awetik' *abełay*	—	Cycle of Gospel scenes (fols. 1b–7b, *see* Appendix C); Letter of Eusebius (fol. 8b); Canon Tables (fols. 10b–14a); Portraits (fols. 14b, 105b, 163b, 268b); Headpieces (fols. 15a, 106a, 164a, 269a).	Later colophons of owners dated 1460 and 1580. A brief notice on fol. 105a written by the scribe asks 'Let God bless Xetrsayn who worked and brought the paper from Halpay [i.e. Aleppo]'.
Awetik' *abełay* Hałbatec'i	—	Headpieces (fols. 72, 126, 218); Portraits (fols. 125b, 217b).	In 1515 the manuscript was at the church of Surb Astuacacin in Edessa; in 1583 the MS was sold in Erzrum, which was acquired by Srapion (later Catholicos of Ējmiacin, 1603–1606) and returned to Edessa. There is a blue stamp bearing the name of the Prelacy of Edessa 1868. This MS was bought of S. Baronian, 9 Nov. 1883. *Cf.* Or.2678; 2679, 2680.
Martiros	—	Portraits (fols. 2b, 80b, 136b, 229b); Headpieces (fols. 3, 81, 137, 230); marginal miniatures (see Appendix B).	In 1730 the MS was repaired and rebound and in 1866, a doctor called Guendurian a native of Mardin sold the MS to Joseph Lilly, who sold it to the library, on 22 April, 1868.
Karapet	—	17 cycle of Gospel scenes (fols. 7b–23b); Letter of Eusebius (fols. 24b–25); Canon Tables (fols. 27–33); Portraits (fols. 34b, 109b, 156b, 234); Headpieces (fols. 35, 110, 157, 235). (*See* Appendix C).	Contains 'Yayl mē vardapetē asac'eal ban vasn xoranac' Awetaranin' (Discourse on the canon tables).
Małak'ia	—	Portraits (fols. 2b, 78b, 122b); Headpieces (fols. 3, 79, 123, 203); Full-page miniatures: *The Crucifixion* (fol. 121a), *Christ Enthroned* (fol. 202b).	*See Christie's valuable early printed books and manuscripts* January 30, 1980. Lot 228.

MS NO	*Conybeare Catalogue No*	*Physical Description*	*Script*	*Date*	*Place*
Add.7940	23, pp. 41–42	Oriental glazed paper; 349 fols.	*bolorgir*	AD 1600	—
Or.5737	24, pp. 42–44	Glossy stout paper; 309 fols.	*bolorgir*	1608	Šoš which is Aspahan (i.e. Isfahan)
Add.19549	22, pp. 39–41	Transparent white vellum; 395 fols.	*bolorgir*	1615	Aleppo
Or.8832	R. Curzon, *Catalogue*, no. 4.	Paper; 311 fols.	*bolorgir*	1630	Istanbul
Or.13895	—	Vellum; 333 fols.	*bolorgir*	1658	Crimea
Or.13808	—	Vellum; 347 fols.	*bolorgir*	17th cent. (1680?)	Constantinople
Or.5449	20, pp. 35–36	Fine vellum; 271 fols.	small *bolorgir*	1683	New Julfa
Or.14161	—	Vellum; 301 fols.	*bolorgir*	1695	Constantinople

Scribe	*Artist*	*Illuminations and Illustrations*	*Remarks*
—	—	16 cycle of Gospel scenes (fols. 1–16, *see* Appendix C); Letter of Eusebius & Canon Tables (fols. 17–26); Portraits (fols. 29b, 120b, 181b, 271b); Headpieces (fols. 30, 121, 182, 272).	There is no principal colophon. On fol. 347 in small current hand Awet Setʿean notes that Petros Setʿean gave the MS to Petros *sarkawag*. On fols. 1, 3, 7, 20b are the stamps of a seal bearing the words 'Melikʿ Simēon 1224 (i.e. 1774)'.
Mesrop *całkoł* Xizancʿi (of Khizan)	—	17 cycle of Gospel scenes (fols. 1b–17a); Letter of Eusebius (fols. 18b–19); Canon Tables (fols. 20b–27a); Portraits (fols. 29b, 105b, 156b, 240b); Headpieces (fols. 30, 106, 157, 241).	In 1618 Mesrop restored the New Testament written in 1280 at Sis and added the portraits of the Evangelists and those of the authors of the Acts and Epistles. See Add.18549. Restored for *xawjay* Nazar, Kālantār of New Julfa, 1618.
Vardan *Lehacʿi* (of Lwow)	Israyel of Amith and Awetikʿ	Letter of Eusebius (fols. 2b–3); Canon Tables (fols. 4b–11a); Portraits (fols. 15b, 117b, 189b, 304b); Headpieces (fols. 16, 118, 190, 305).	Written for *xawjay* Sanos Čʿelebi and presented to the church of the Forty Martyrs at Aleppo, which Sanos and his brother *xawjay* Petros had re-endowed in 1615. A letter at the beginning from its last owner assigns the MS to the 11th or 12th century.
Mkrtičʿ *sarkawag*	—	Headpieces (fols. 1, 79, 136, 236); Portraits (fols. 135b, 235b).	The portraits of St Mark (fol. 78b) and St Matthew (fol. 1b) are left blank. A note in English on the inside of the front cover reads 'R. Curzon bought of an Armenian priest, at Constantinople, 1837'.
Nikołayos *całkarar*	—	12 cycle of Gospel scenes (fols. 4b–15a); Letter of Eusebius (fols. 16b–17a); Canon Tables (fols. 18b–25b); Portraits (fols. 28b, 112b, 169b, 263b); Headpieces (fols. 29a, 113a, 170a, 264a).	The MS is bound in wooden boards encased in silver, the work of the silversmith Ełiay dated 1755/6. The front with the *Transfiguration*, the back with the *Entry into Jerusalem* in relief. Both scenes are inspired by the miniatures in the text depicting the same scenes on fols. 8b & 9a.
—	—	Canon Tables (fols. 3b–8a,11b–12a); Letter of Eusebius (fols. 9b–10a); Portraits (fols. 16b, 109b, 172b, 264b); Headpieces (fols. 17, 110, 173, 265); 56 marginal illustrations.	Bound in parcel gilt repoussé the upper cover depicting the *Nativity*, with an inscription from St Luke, the lower cover representing the *Ressurrection*, the spine ornamented with portraits of prophets. It is the work of silversmith Malxas Hači of Caesarea, dated 1691. *See REA*, VI (1926), pp. 27–31.
—	—	16 cycle of Gospel scenes (fols. 1b–16a see Appendix C); Letter of Eusebius to Carpianus (fols. 17b–18a); Canon Tables (fols. 19b–26a); Portraits (fols. 29b, 98b, 144b, 217b); Headpieces (fols. 30, 99, 145, 218); 52 marginal illustrations.	In Conybeare the date given is 1582. The two figures in the picture of the *Mystic* Cross (fol. 15b) are the owners of the MS, 'Ałavali' and 'Xanpʿari'.
Xačʿatur	Gabriēl *całkoł*	16 cycle of Gospel scenes (fols. 1b–16a); Letter of Eusebius (fols. 17b–18a); Canon Tables (fols. 19b–26a); Portraits (fols. 30b, 106b, 158b, 241b); Headpieces (fols. 31, 107, 159, 242); 50 marginal illustrations.	This Gabriel is the artist of MS 319 in Vienna, who names his father as Markos *patkerahan* ('portraitist'). Belonged to William III, King of England, Scotland and Ireland 1688–1702, then to Marquess of Bute in 1873.

APPENDIX B

Subject analysis of the marginal miniatures in British Library manuscripts

The marginal miniatures in Armenian Gospel-books stand as a visual commentary on the text. The choice of the text for illustration is determined by the desire to comment on specific texts of exegetical importance. The density of the programme varies. Byzantine manuscripts illustrate St Matthew fully and then fill in only the new subjects in the other gospels, while in Armenian practice each gospel has its own programme with no effort made to eliminate repetition: for example, the Crucifixion is illustrated twice in Add. MS 27489 (fols. 69b, 111a), the two blind men of Jericho in Or.15411 (fols. 61b, 217b), and the Burial of Christ in Or.5304 (fols. 23b, 68b). There are certain themes that are of special significance and commonly receive a pictorial treatment, such as the Annunciation, Entry into Jerusalem, and the Wedding at Cana (the first miracle through which Christ's divine power became manifest). A few animals drawn in the margins are not mere ornaments, but are related to the text. A sheep may accompany Christ's word: 'I am the good shepherd'; two small birds may illustrate the pericope of the Presentation of Christ in the Temple (Or.5761, fol. 62a); a bird with a fish in its beak illustrates Christ's appearance to the apostles when He ate 'a piece of broiled fish' (Or.5737, fols. 301a, 301b, 302b). A small temple may accompany the reference to the Temple or to the city of Jerusalem; a tree serves as illustration for the barren tree cursed by Christ; ears of corn illustrate the story of the lawfulness of working on the Sabbath (*Matthew 12:1*), and the bowl of fire to depict the saying 'I came to cast fire'.

The representations are often reduced to one or two figures at most, and in some instances to a single element of the story; for example, instead of a scene showing the beheading of John the Baptist, often his head on a platter alone is represented (Or.2679, fol. 96b); for the Entry into Jerusalem a colt tied to a tree is shown (Or.82, fol. 206b); and a cock on its own represents the story of Peter's denial (Or.5761, fols. 74a, 128, 198a).

There is not always an exact correspondence between the text of a given verse and the image that accompanies it. This discrepancy can be explained by the fact that the passage illustrated may occur in the inner column of text while the image has to be painted in the outer margin.

The following is a comprehensive analysis of all the marginal miniatures in Armenian manuscripts in the British Library.

Or.2679. Canton of Arčeš, AD 1281

Fol.	*Subject*	*Text*
	St Matthew	
63b	The Temple	*24:1–2*
81b	A frontal standing figure of St Mary 'Surb koysn Mariam' written above in the inner blank margin	
	St Mark	
89a	A ram	*?*
96b	The head of John the Baptist	*6:14–15*
97b	Jesus with a walking stick	*6:30–31*
109b	A ram	*10:6–8*
112b	A fig tree and two busts	*10:46–47*
115a	The Temple	*11:27–28*
119a	The Temple	*13:1–2*
131b	Full frontal standing portrait of St Luke in the outer margin	
	St Luke	
134a	The angel Gabriel	*1:30–31*
134b	The Virgin Mary	*1:39–40*
137b	A shepherd boy playing the flute	*2:8–9*
138b	Presentation in the temple. A temple with two doves perched on the columns	*2:22–23*
198a	A fig tree	*18:35–36*
	St John	
224a	A ram	*1:29–30*
254a	The Temple	*10:22–23*
277a	An ornate cross	
280a	An ornate cross	*19:17–18*

Or.10960. T'oros of Vahka, Gřner, AD 1295

Fol.	*Subject*	*Text*
	St Matthew	
12a	Jesus and the two blind men	*9:27*
22a	A temple	*12:43–45*
27b	Jesus sitting on a donkey and a palm tree in the background	*21:5–6*
28b	A fig tree	*21:18–19*
32b	The Temple, with altar and a chalice placed on it	*24:1–2*

	St Mark	
50b	John the Baptist kneeling in front of a soldier with raised sword	6:27–28
52a	Three disciples sitting in a boat	8:10–11
59a	A palm tree with Bartimaeus climbing	10:46–47
62b	The Temple	13:1–2
	St Luke	
73b	Presentation in the temple. Simēon's bust within the columns of a temple; two doves perched on the initial letter 'E'	2:25–26
90b	'Now he was casting out a demon that was dumb'. The demon is represented as a black winged figure coming out of the man and the hand of God is placed above the figure	11:1–2
92b	'Teacher, bid my brother divide the inheritance with me'. Christ is depicted in full frontal figure, with the brother on a slightly lower position pointing to a bowl containing coins	12:14–15
94a	A bowl of fire	12:49–50
101b	The Pharisee and the tax-collector at prayer, the hand of God above the figures	18:10–11
102a	The blind man of Jericho, the hand of God above	18:35–36
103b	A palm tree	19:29–30
106a	The Temple	21:5–6
	St John	
116a	Marriage at Cana; a servant pours water into a jug with Jesus looking on	2:1
118a	Jesus sitting beside the well, with the woman of Samaria drawing water	4:6–7
129b	The Temple	10:22–23
135b	An altar covered with a cloth upon which is placed a chalice and immediately above it the holy spirit descends upon it in the shape of a dove with nimbus 'And I will pray the Father, and he will give you another counsellor'	14:15–18

Add. MS27489. Cilician, 13–14th century

Fol.	*Subject*	*Text*
	St Matthew	
51a	A palm tree and a dove descending on it	20:29–30
52b	A cup	21:18
69b	The Crucifixion	27:1–2
	St Mark	
100a	The Temple	11:27–28
103b	The Temple	13:1–2
111a	The Crucifixion	15:1–2
	St Luke	
119b	The angel Gabriel	1:26

Note: Fols. 139 to end by another hand and lack marginal miniatures

Add. MS15411. T'oros of Tarōn, Gladjor, AD 1321

Fol.	*Subject*	*Text*
	St Matthew	
14a	John the Baptist, holding a cross and an open scroll	3:1–2
30b	The two blind men	9:27
50b	The Temple	16:7–20
60b	The Temple	20:17–18
61b	The two blind men of Jericho	20:30
63b	A fig tree	21:18–19
71b	The Temple	24:1–2
79a	Ewer with cup	26:18
83b	A cross	27:1–3
	St Mark	
126b	Bartimaeus the blind beggar	10:46–47
128a	A fig tree	11:12–13
129b	The Temple	11:27
133a	The Temple	12:35
134a	The Temple	13:3
143a	A cross with a crown above it	14:1–2
	St Luke	
154b	A shepherd and two sheep	2:8
155b	The Temple	2:22–23
157a	The Temple	2:41–42
216a	A child holding an open scroll	18:17–18
217b	The blind beggar of Jericho	18:35–36
220a	A tree	19:31
225b	The Temple	21:5–6
	St John	
244a	'The lamb of God'	1:29–30
246a	The bride and groom sitting under a canopy, with seven jars of water	2:5–6
247b	The Temple	2:19–20
252b	A dove	4:24–25
255a	The Temple	5:1–2
258a	A stag	
259a	An eagle	
271b	The man who was blind from birth	9:1–2
282b	Entry into Jerusalem. A boy holding a palm branch	12:12–14
289a	A dove	14:11–12
302b	Jesus holding a cross and a scroll	19:17–18
307b	A fish	21:1–3

Or.82. Martiros of Khizan, 15th century

Fol.	*Subject*	*Text*
	St Matthew	
50b	The two blind men of Jericho and Jesus	20:29–30
52a	A fig tree	21:18–19
	St Mark	
111b	Bartimaeus the blind beggar and Jesus	10:46
112b	A fig tree	11:12–13
	St Luke	
140a	Mary and Elizabeth	1:39–40
143a	Shepherd, and sheep grazing	2:8–9
171b	Christ praying	11:1–2
181a	Candlestick	11:33
204a	The blind man of Jericho and Jesus	18:35–36
206b	A colt tied to a tree	19:28–29
211b	The Temple	21:5–6

St John

233b	Jesus and the jars of water at Cana	*2:1–2*
242a	Jesus and the paralytic at Bethesda	*5:5–6*
257b	Jesus healing the man blind from birth	*9:1–3*
287a	Jesus carrying his cross	*19:17–18*

Or.13895. Nikołayos of Crimea, AD 1658

Fol.	*Subject*	*Text*
	St Matthew	
29a	The Tree of Jesse: Jesse lies prone on the ground with hand raised holding from the meandering scroll, which frames the busts of David, Abraham, and the Virgin; with Christ's full-figure placed above.	*1:1–2*
30b	Joseph's dream	*1:18*
31a	The three Magi (rubbed)	*2:1–2*
33a	Christ	*2:23*
35b	John the Baptist	*4:12*
36b	Jesus and two men from the crowd	*5:1–2*
37b	Jesus and a man from the crowd	*5:17–18*
40a	Jesus	*6:1*
42a	Jesus	*6:22*
43a	Jesus and a man	*7:1–2*
46b	Jesus and three men	*8:18–19*
48a	Jesus and Matthew kneeling	*9:9*
49a	Jesus and the ruler who 'knelt before him'	*9:18*
49b	Two blind men kneeling	*9:27*
50a	Jesus	*9:35*
51b	Jesus and two disciples (the disciples have haloes)	*10:16*
53b	Jesus	*11:1–2*
55a	Jesus	*11:1–2*
55b	Jesus	*12:1–2*
57a	Jesus healing the blind and dumb demoniac; the demon is shown coming out of the man's mouth	*12:22*
58a	Jesus and two men	*12:37–38*
59b	Jesus	*13:1*
61a	Jesus	*13:24*
62a	Jesus and two disciples	*13:36–37*
63b	Jesus	*13:53–54*
64a	King Herod seated on a throne	*14:1–2*
64b	Jesus	*14:13*
65a	Three disciples in a boat	*14:22–23*
66a	Jesus and two men	*15:1–2*
67a	Jesus and the Canaanite woman	*15:22*
68a	Jesus	*15:29*
69b	Jesus and two disciples	*16:13*
72a	Jesus and the man who came up to him and kneeling before him	*17:14–15*
72b	Jesus and two disciples	*17:21–22*
74a	Jesus	*18:10*
76a	Jesus	*19:1*
77a	Jesus and the man who said 'Teacher, what good . . .'	*19:16*
79b	Jesus and two disciples	*20:17–18*
80b	Jesus and the two blind men of Jericho	*20:29–30*
82a	Jesus standing under the fig-tree	*21:18–19*
83b	Jesus and a man	*21:33*
85a	Jesus	*22:1–2*
86a	Two Pharisees	*22:15*
87b	Jesus and three men	*23:1–2*
90b	The Temple and Jesus standing next to it	*24:1–2*
97b	Three men	*26:3–4*
98b	Jesus and two disciples	*26:17–18*
99b	Jesus and two disciples	*26:30–31*
101b	Jesus before Caiaphus the high priest	*26:57*
103a	Three chief priests	*27:1–2*
107a	Joseph of Arimathea kneeling	*27:57*
107b	Pilate and a man	*27:58*
108a	Mary Magdalene and the other Mary	*28:1–2*
	St Mark	
114a	Jesus	*1:14–15*
115a	Jesus and two men	*1:21*
115b	Jesus and two disciples (John and James)	*1:29*
116b	Jesus and the paralytic man laying on a bed	*2:3–4*
117b	Jesus and Levi son of Alphaeus	*2:14*
118b	Two disciples	*2:23*
119b	Pharisees and Herodians (four figures)	*3:6*
120a	Jesus standing on a mountain and gathered around him five disciples	*3:13–14*
120b	Jesus and a man	*3:21–22*
121a	Jesus and a man	*3:31–32*
121b	Jesus	*4:1–2*
122a	Jesus with two disciples	*4:10–11*
123a	Jesus and a man (1)	*4:21–22*
	Jesus and a man (2)	*4:26–27*
124a	Jesus and three men	*4:35–36*
126a	Jesus and Jairus at his feet	*5:22–23*
127a	Jesus with Jairus kneeling at His feet and the messenger	*5:35–36*
127b	Jesus with three disciples	*6:1–2*
128a	Jesus and three disciples	*6:7–8*
128b	King Herod seated on a throne with a man standing before him	*6:14–15*
130a	Jesus and three disciples	*6:30–31*
131a	The three disciples in the boat	*6:45*
132a	Jesus and two men	*7:1–2*
133b	Jesus and two disciples	*7:17–18*
134b	Jesus and the deaf man	*7:32–33*
135a	Jesus with two disciples	*8:1–2*
135b	Jesus with three disciples	*8:10–11*
137a	Jesus with two disciples	*8:27*
139a	The crowd (five figures grouped)	*9:13–14*
140a	Jesus with three disciples	*9:29–30*
141b	Jesus	*10:1–2*
142b	Jesus with two children at His feet	*10:13–14*
143b	Jesus and Peter	*10:28–29*
144a	Jesus with a group of disciples (3 figures)	*10:33*
145b	Jesus and Bartimaeus, a blind beggar	*10:46*
147a	Jesus standing under the fig-tree	*11:12*
148a	Jesus and three men	*11:27–28*
149b	Jesus and two Saducees	*12:18*
151a	Jesus	*12:35*
152a	The Temple with Jesus standing next to it	*13:1*

155a	Jesus and the women with an alabaster jar of pure nard	14:3–4
156a	Jesus and two disciples	14:12–13
157a	Jesus and two disciples	14:27–28
161a	Jesus before Pilate seated on a throne	15:1–2
164a	Joseph of Arimathea kneeling	15:42–43
165b	Jesus appears to Mary Magdalene	16:9–10

St Luke

172a	Annunciation: Mary and the angel Gabriel	1:26
173a	The Virgin Mary	1:39
175b	A soldier holding up the decree of Augustus	2:1–2
176a	Shepherds (two) keeping watch over their flock and the angel in a segment of sky	2:8–9
177a	Circumcision: the high priest holds Jesus with Joseph standing by	2:21
	Presentation in the temple: Joseph holding two doves with Mary along side him	2:22–23
178b	Jesus	2:41
179b	Pontius Pilate	3:1
183b	Jesus	4:14
184b	Jesus	4:31
185b	Jesus	4:43
187a	Jesus and the man with 'full of leprosy'	5:12
187b	Jesus standing over the man who was paralysed laying in bed	5:18–19
188b	Jesus and Levi kneeling	5:27
189b	Two disciples	6:1–2
190b	Jesus praying	6:12
193b	Jesus	7:1–2
194b	Jesus blessing the man who had died and her mother kneeling at the foot of Jesus	7:12–13
197a	Jesus sitting with a Pharisee	7:36–37
198a	Jesus	8:1–2
200a	Three disciples in the boat	8:22–23
203a	Jesus with three disciples	9:1–2
204b	Jesus	9:18
206a	Jesus and a man (Jairus)	9:37–38
207b	Jesus	9:51
208a	A group of disciples (5 figures)	10:1–2
210a	Jesus and a lawyer	10:25
211b	Jesus and a disciple	11:1–2
212b	Jesus casting out a demon that was dumb	11:14
214b	Jesus	11:33
217a	Jesus and a man	12:13
218b	Jesus	12:32
220a	Jesus	12:49
221b	Jesus	13:10
222b	Jesus	13:22
224a	Jesus and the man who had dropsy	14:2–3
226a	Jesus and two men	14:25–26
229a	Jesus with two disciples	16:1–2
232a	Jesus with two disciples	17:1–2
233b	Jesus and a Pharisee	17:20
234b	Jesus	18:1–2
235b	Jesus blessing two children	18:15
237a	Jesus and the blind man from Jericho	18:35
239b	Two disciples	19:29
241a	Jesus and two men	20:1–2
242a	Jesus and a disciple	20:9–10
243b	Jesus and two Saducees	20:27
245a	Jesus and a man	21:5
247b	Jesus and a man	22:1–2
249a	Jesus and a man	22:21–22
252b	The Chief priest and a scribe	22:66
256b	Joseph of Arimathea	23:50–51
258a	Two disciples and Jesus on the road to Emmaus	24:13–14
259b	Jesus among two disciples	24:36
260a	Jesus and two of his disciples	24:43–44

St John

265a	Jesus	1:18
266a	Jesus and John the Baptist	1:29–30
267a	Jesus and Philip	1:43
268a	Marriage at Cana, a servant with jar pours water into a jar; six jars in rows of three with Jesus standing over them; below the steward is shown seated and a servant offering him a jar	2:1–2
268a	Jesus	2:12
269b	Jesus	2:23
269b	Jesus	3:13
270b	A group of disciples	3:22–23
271b	Jesus	4:1–2
273a	Jesus and the Samaritan woman	4:24–25
274b	Jesus	4:43
275b	Jesus and the man who was ill for thirty years	5:1–2
276b	Jesus and two men	5:19
277b	Jesus and a man	5:31–32
279a	Jesus	6:1
280a	Jesus	6:15
280b	Three disciples in the boat	6:22
281b	Jesus	6:39
284a	Jesus	7:1
284b	Jesus	7:14
286a	Jesus	7:24
287a	Jesus	7:37
288a	Jesus	8:1–2
288b	Jesus with two men	8:21
289b	Jesus with three men	8:31
291b	Jesus and the man who was blind from birth	9:1
294b	Jesus	9:39
295b	Jesus	10:11
296a	Jesus	10:22
297b	The Raising of Lazarus: Jesus standing while Mary and Martha prostrate at His feet and to the left of them Lazarus in a cave	11:1–2
300a	The chief priest and Pharisees	11:47
301a	Three men	11:55
302a	Jesus	12:12
303a	Jesus	12:24
303b	Jesus	12:27
304b	Jesus	12:44
305a	Jesus	13:1–2
306b	Jesus and two men	13:16
307b	Jesus	13:31
309a	Jesus and two men	14:15
309b	Jesus and two men	14:25
316b	Judas	18:2–3

319a	Jesus with hand tied led by a soldier into the house of Caiaphus	18:28
321b	Jesus bearing his own cross	19:17
323a	Joseph of Arimathea	19:38
325a	Jesus among the disciples (two figures)	20:19–20
325b	Jesus	20:26
326a	Jesus with Simeon and Thomas	21:1–2
327a	Jesus and Simeon	21:15

Or.13808. Constantinople, AD 1680

Fol.	*Subject*	*Text*
	ST MATTHEW	
16b & 17a	Ancestors of Christ: six busts of men within medalions in the outer margins	1:8–15
19b	The three Magi, with golden crowns and bearing gifts	2:1–2
20b	Flight into Egypt: Mary with the child seated on donkey	2:13–14
22b	John the Baptist holding an open scroll	3:11–12
38b	Jesus calling St Matthew	9:9–10
39b	Jesus and the ruler (Jairus)	9:18
40b	Jesus healing the two blind men	9:27–28
52a	Jesus and the crowd	13:3–4
57a	The head of John the Baptist on a platter	14:4–5
61a	Jesus and the woman of Canaan	15:21–22
63b	Jesus and a disciple	16:13–14
66a	Jesus and the man who had an epileptic son	17:14–15
71b	Jesus and the man who said 'Teacher, what good . . .'	19:16
74a	Jesus and a disciple	20:17–18
75b	Jesus healing the two blind men of Jericho	20:29
77a	A fig tree	21:18–19
81a	Jesus and one of the Herodians	22:15–16
86b	The Temple	24:1–2
98a	Jesus being led away by a soldier	26:57–58
99b	Jesus carrying his cross	27:1–2
103b	Joseph of Arimathea	27:57–58
104a	The chief priest and two soldiers	27:62–63
104b	Mary at the sepulchre	28:1
	ST MARK	
112a	Jesus and the man with unclean spirit	1:23
113a	Jesus and the leper	1:40
113b	Jesus and the paralytic man on a bed	2:3–4
114b	Jesus calling Levi the son of Alphaeus	2:13–14
117b	Jesus and Simeon	3:16–17
118b	Jesus and his mother	3:31–32
119b	Jesus and a disciple	4:10–11
121b	Jesus sitting in the stern of a boat	4:38–39
123b	Jesus and Jairus	5:21–22
124b	Jesus and the messenger	5:35–36
130b	Jesus and a disciple	7:17–18
131b	Jesus and the dumb and blind man	7:32–33
133a	Jesus and a Pharisee	8:11
134b	Jesus and two disciples	8:27–28
137a	Jesus and the man who had a son with dumb spirit	9:17–18
140a	Jesus and a Pharisee	10:2–3
141a	Jesus blessing a child	10:13
143a	Jesus with James and John	10:35
146a	A fig tree in leaf	11:13
158a	Jesus and Simeon Peter	14:29
162a	Jesus with hands tied behind his back stands before Pilate who is seated on a throne	15:1–2
	ST LUKE	
174b	The angel Gabriel	1:19–20
175a	St Mary	1:26–27
176a	Mary and Elizabeth	1:39–40
179a	The Nativity: Mary and the child in a cave, Joseph on one side of the cave with the angel above and a group of saints	2:8–9
190a	Jesus healing the man full of leprosy	5:12–13
200a	Jesus and a Pharisee	7:36–37
213a	Jesus and the lawyer	10:25
215b	Jesus casting out a demon that was dumb	11:14
224a	Jesus healing the woman who had infirmity	13:10–11
237b	Jesus blessing a child	18:15
238a	Jesus and the blind man of Jericho	18:35
243a	Jesus and the chief priest	20:1–2
245a	Jesus and a Sadducee	20:27
246b	The Temple	21:5–6
257a	Joseph of Arimathea	23:50
	ST JOHN	
269b	Jesus	2:12
285b	The Temple	7:14
293a	Jesus healing the man who was blind from birth	9:1–2
323b	Joseph of Arimathea asking Pilate for the body of Jesus	19:38

Or.5737. Mesrop of Khizan, Šoš, AD 1608

Fol.	*Subject*	*Text*
	ST MATTHEW	
31b	Joseph sleeping, above him the angel	1:20–21
32a	The three wise men	2:1–2
33b	John the Baptist holding a scroll	3:1–3
79a	The vineyard and set a hedge and tower	21:33–34
85a	The Temple	24:1–3
93b	A sheep	26:32–33
95b	A cock	26:75
97a	A cross	27:1–2
101b	Mary and Mary Magdalene at the sepulchre	28:1–2
	ST MARK	
119b	A soldier carrying the head of John the Baptist on a platter resting on his head	6:27–28
136a	A fig tree	11:12–13
141a	The Temple	13:1–3
152a	Joseph of Arimathea	42–43
	ST LUKE	
159a	The angel Gabriel	1:26–27
163a	Presentation in the temple: a temple with two doves	2:23–24
164a	The Temple	2:41–42
195b	Bowl of fire 'No one after lighting a lamb'	11:33–34
200b	Bowl of fire 'I came to cast fire'	12:49
224a	The Temple	21:1–2
234b	Joseph of Arimathea	23:50–51

	St John	
243a	'The lamb of God'	*1:29–30*
247a	A cross the horizontal arm of which is formed by a serpent: 'As Moses lifted up the serpent . . .'	*3:13–14*
252b	The sheep gate with five porticoes	*5:1–4*
301a	Three fishes: 'Children have you any fish'	*21:1–4*
301b	A fish on a plate 'charcoal fire, with fish lying on it'	*21:9–8*
302b	A fish in a bowl: 'Bring some of the fish'	*21:10*

Or.5449. New Julfa, AD 1683

Fol.	*Subject*	*Text*
	St Matthew	
32a	Three Magi bearing gifts	*2:2–3*
47a	Christ and the two blind men kneeling	*9:27*
52a	Cornfield	*12:1–2*
53a	Jesus and the blind and dumb demoniac kneeling	*12:22*
57b	Jesus and a disciple	*13:36–37*
70a	Jesus and the rich young man	*19:16*
71b	The Temple	*20:17–18*
80b	The Temple	*24:1–2*
94b	Joseph of Arimathea	*27:57–58*
	St Mark	
103b	A bunch of ears of corn in a bowl	*2:23*
106a	Jesus and a disciple	*4:10–11*
124b	Jesus and Bartimaeus, the blind beggar, kneeling	*10:46–47*
126a	A fig tree	*11:13*
126b	The Temple	*11:27*
130a	The Temple	*13:1–2*
138a	A cross	*15:20*
139b	Joseph of Arimathea	*15:42–43*
	St Luke	
147b	Annunciation: Mary and Elizabeth	*1:39*
149b	Annunciation to the shepherd: the angel hovering above the head of a shepherd 'keeping watch over the flock'	*2:8*
156b	Christ and the demoniac	*4:33–34*
158a	Christ and the man full of leprosy	*5:12*
159b	Christ and the calling of Levi	*5:27*
160a	Cornfield	*6:1–2*
165b	Jesus and a Pharisee	*7:36*
170b	Jesus and two apostles	*9:1*
178a	Christ and the dumb demon	*11:14*
179a	A lamp	*11:33*
183b	Flames rising from a bowl	*12:49*
185a	Jesus and the woman who had had a spirit of infirmity kneeling	*13:10*
185b	The Temple	*13:22*
196a	Jesus blessing two children	*18:15*
197a	Jesus and the blind man from Jericho	*18:35*
202a	Jesus and a Sadducee	*20:27*
211b	Joseph of Arimathea	*23:50*
	St John	
222a	The Temple	*2:23*
223a	Jesus and the serpent raised on a rod	*3:13–14*
228a	The Temple	*5:1–2*
230b	Jesus and two apostles	*6:1–2*
235b	The Temple	*7:14*
236b	Jesus teaching	*7:37*
240b	Jesus and the man born blind	*9:1*
251a	Jesus and a man standing before Him	*12:44*
265a	Christ bearing the cross	*19:17*
266b	Joseph of Arimathea	*19:38*

Or.14161. Gabriēl *całkoł*, Constantinople, AD 1695

Fol.	*Subject*	*Text*
	St Matthew	
31a	Ancestors of Christ: 12 busts of men in the meanders of a scroll, with the bust of the Virgin and Child in the uppermost medallion	*1:8–16*
34a	Joseph's dream and angel	*1:20–21*
34b	John the Baptist with wings and holding an open scroll	*3:1–2*
46b	Jesus and the scribe	*8:18–19*
48a	Jesus and Matthew the tax collector	*9:9–10*
48b	Jesus and the ruler 'who knelt before him'	*9:18*
49a	Jesus healing the two blind men	*9:27*
54b	Jesus thanking his Father 'Lord of Heaven' represented by the sun	*11:25*
55a	Ears of corn	*12:1–2*
56a	Jesus healing the blind and dumb demoniac	*12:22*
66a	Jesus and the Canaanite woman	*15:21*
70a	Jesus and the man who had an epileptic son	*17:14*
74b	Jesus and the man who said 'Teacher, what good deed . . .'	*19:16*
77b	Jesus healing the two blind men sitting by the roadside	*20:29*
95a	Jesus and Peter	*26:34–36*
98a	Judas hanging from a tree, with the demon and the coins at the foot of the tree	*27:5–6*
101b	Joseph of Arimathea	*27:57*
	St Mark	
108b	Jesus healing the 'man with an unclean spirit'	*1:21–23*
111a	Jesus calling Levi son of Alphaeus	*2:13–14*
111b	Ears of corn	*2:23–24*
113a	Jesus seated with 'those whom he desired'	*3:13–14*
119a	Jesus and the ruler (Jairus)	*5:35–36*
126a	Jesus healing the man who was deaf and dumb	*7:32–33*
133a	Jesus and a child	*10:13–14*
136a	Jesus and Bartimaeus, a blind beggar	*10:46–47*
137a	Jesus under a 'fig tree in leaf'	*11:12–13*
146b	Jesus and Peter	*14:29–30*
153a	Joseph of Arimathea	*15:42–43*
	St Luke	
161a	Annunciation: the angel Gabriel and the Virgin Mary	*1:26*
164a	A shepherd boy with hat in hand, looking up to an angel above his head, and below sheep grazing	2:8–9
171b	Jesus healing the man with an unclean demon	*4:33–34*
173b	Jesus healing the man full of leprosy	*5:12*
175a	Jesus and Levi, the tax collector	*5:27–28*
175b	Ears of corn	*6:1–2*
176b	Jesus kneeling in prayer	*6:12*

179b	Jesus and the centurion	7:1–3
182a	Jesus and a woman(?)	7:36–37
186b	Jesus and Jairus	8:41–42
190b	Jesus and the man whose son was possessed by a demon	9:37–38
194a	Jesus and the lawyer	10:25–26
196b	Jesus casting out a demon that was dumb	11:14
200b	Jesus and one of the brothers	12:13–14
203a	Jesus standing over a bowl of fire: 'I came to cast fire'	12:49
204b	Jesus healing the woman who had infirmity	13:11–12
223b	Jesus and a Saducee	20:27
234b	Joseph of Arimathea	23:50
	St John	
243b	John the Baptist, holding 'the lamb of God'	1:29–30
245b	Jesus blessing the six jars at the marriage at Cana	2:1
248a	Moses raising the serpent on the cross	3:14
256b	Jesus and Philip	6:7
262b	Jesus and a man	7:24–25
263b	Jesus 'stood up and proclaimed'	7:37
264b	Jesus and a man	8:12–13
267b	Jesus and the man who was blind from birth	9:1
271a	Jesus and a disciple	10:11–12
272b	The Raising of Lazarus	11:1–2
277a	Entry into Jerusalem: Jesus and a child holding a palm branch	12:12–13
283a	Jesus and a disciple	14:15–16
296b	Joseph of Arimathea	19:38
300a	Jesus and Simon Peter	21:15

Or.5304. Awag *całkoł*, AD 1329/58

Fol.	*Subject*	*Text*
	St Matthew	
9b	LBM. Joseph's dream. Joseph reclining with the angel descending on him from above. Outlined in red with slight colour. The gold for the nimbus's of the angel and Joseph rubbed.	1:18–19
10a	TLC. The slaughter of the Innocents (5.6 × 6 cm). Text interrupted at 2:16 'in Bethlehem and in all that region' and resumed 'he had ascertained from the wise men'. Henceforth I shall indicate this with a /.	
	TRM. A tree	2:8–9
	BRC. Baptism of Christ. Red border, St John Baptist, bearded and in brown robe, tall and looking up. Christ centre fronted, in water, with nimbus and red loin cloth, standing in water. At the top, the hand of God, and the Holy Spirit as a dove descending. Right, two angels, with elaborate red wings. Picture inserted at the conclusion of 3:17 'This is my beloved son with whom I am well pleased'.	
10b	TRC. Jesus calls the two brothers. Jesus standing on the ground facing James and John who are standing in the boat, while Zebedee their father is seated rowing the boat. 4:21 'and he called them'/22 'Immediately they left the boat and their father, and followed him'.	
11b	TLM. A candlestick with three flames	6:22–23
12b	BLC. Jesus meets the two demoniacs of Gadarenes. Jesus approaches from the left towards the two demoniacs coming out of the tombs. 8:28 'coming out of the tombs'/'so fierce that no one . . .'.	
15b	BLC. Christ feeding the multitudes. Christ standing (outlined in red) approaches the crowd of ten men and women seated in rows of two and threes. 14:19 'and taking the five loaves and two/fish'.	
	MRC. Jesus walking on the sea. Jesus wearing blue gown over red walks on the sea towards a boat carrying the disciples. The gold of the background has come off. 14:25 'came to them walking on the sea/26 'But when the disciples . . .'.	
16b	RBC. The Transfiguration (10 × 6 cm). Christ with Moses and Elijah standing on three mountain peaks, Moses holding the tablet, shown in red outline. The three disciples below sprawled against purple rocks. All have haloes. 17:2 'And he was transfigured before them/and his face shone . . .'.	
18b–19a	Upper middle spread across the two inside columns. The Entry into Jerusalem (12 × 16 cm). Christ on donkey, left, moving right, the animal well delineated anatomically in red. Disciples with haloes, crowded behind Christ on left. To the right four elders (feint) stand outside the gate of the city and in the foreground three small children spread their garments under the feet of the donkey. 21:8 'spread them on the road/9 'and the crowds'.	
22a	BRC. The Garden of Gethsemane. Christ in blue robe over brown, prostrates at upper right horizontally facing right; two disciples in the top left are shown sleeping with heads resting on their hands and the third disciple is slightly positioned below left also sleeping. The ground is covered with tiny flowers and grass. 26:39 'And going a little farther he fell on his face and prayed/My father'.	
23a	TLC. Pilate washes his hands. Pilate on the left of the picture, with a servant in green robe facing him, pouring water over his hands from a ewer. V-shaped damage. 27:24 'he took water and washed his hands before the crowd/saying I am innocent'.	
	BLC. Woes of parents for their children. A woman on the left wearing red robe and two men on the right stand with one hand raised and placed on their forehead and the other hand resting on the heads of three children. 27:25 '. . . and on our children/26 'Then he released'. Four lines of text separate the two pictures.	
23b	BLC. The Burial of Christ. Christ's body wrapped in white linen with his head to the left, with Joseph and Nicodemus on the right holding His legs and body lowering the body into the open tomb. Mary Magdalene and the other Mary are looking into the tomb from behind a cliff. Cf. with the Burial scene of fol. 68b in St John's Gospel. 27:60 'and laid it in his own new tomb/which he had hewn'.	
	RBC. The Resurrection. The empty tomb is in the foreground with the linen cloth lying in the tomb (Jn.20:6). Above the tomb to the left stand the three women facing the angel on the right with wings spread and cross staff. Below, the empty tomb two soldiers prostrate with their swords and spears thrown around their bodies. 28:4 'the guards trembled and became like dead men/5 'But the angel answered'.	
	St Mark	
25b	Full-page portrait of St Mark	
26a	Rectangular Headpiece	

Abbreviations
B Bottom C Column L Left M Margin R Right T Top
e.g. LBM = Left bottom margin

27a BLC. The healing of the paralytic. Two men on the roof of a house are lowering the paralytic placed in a pallet held by ropes on each end. Inside the house Jesus stands on the left together with three onlookers squatting in the right of the picture. 2:4 'they let down the pallet on which the paralytic lay/5 'And when Jesus saw'.

33b BLC. The anointing of Jesus. Jesus sits to the left, with gold halo, and blue gown over red, while 'a woman with an alabaster jar' stands to the left emptying a red phial over Jesus's head. The gilt background to this miniature has mostly held. 14:3 'and she broke the jar and poured it over his head/4 'but the disciples . . .'.

ST LUKE

35b–36a Blank

36b Full-page portrait of St Luke

37a Headpiece of St Luke. Stepped niche with the miniature of the Virgin and child on the top step under a circular dome, with angels on either side. Below on the third step the busts of Abraham (left) and John the Baptist (right). Below beneath the feet of the Virgin two kneeling figures; a woman on the left and a man on the right holding circular drums. The calf the symbol of the Evangelist forms the initial letter and a floral palmette adorns the outer margin. The text is of latter hand.

37b LBC. The Annunciation (6 × 10 cm). The angel stands to the left with elaborate wings points with right hand towards Mary, who stands to the right in brown over white robe, with slightly undulating stance, under a column. Classical disposition of the picture, but the features of the faces appear to have been crudely re-inked particularly St Mary's. 1:28 'came to her and said "Hail, O favoured one/ the Lord is with you"'.

38b Full-page miniature of the Nativity, with Adoration of the Magi, and 22 lines of text in the top left column. In the TLM a horseman with trumpet, below the text, and slightly left of centre of page, blue oval mandorla with recumbent Virgin, in gold over white, leaning on her right arm, with head to the left looking down. Above her in gold manger, Christ child in red robe, with nimbus, looking to the right, where ox and ass lean over the stall. Top right, choir of angels in rows of five & four (below). Centre right, the three kings with crown each bearing their gifts approach the Virgin from the right into the rocky cave. Bottom left margin shepherd minds his sheep with two angels above them. Two midwives, with haloes bath the baby in a stoup and in the right hand corner Joseph sits in dejection. 2:7 'wrapped him in swaddling cloths, and laid/him in a manger' (fol. 39a col. 1).

39a Presentation of Christ in the Temple (13 × 7 cm). The temple is shown as a tall columned building with round-headed arches. Mary and Joseph stand to the left, Joseph holding two doves in his hand, while Mary has just handed the child Christ to Simeon, who stands centre right on the other side of the altar holding the Child, with long and grave features. Anna the Prophetess is standing behind Simeon. The gilding rubbed. 2:28 'he took him up in his arms/and blessed God and said'.

41a LTM. Ear of corn *6:1–2*

43b CRC. The Raising of Jairus's daughter. Christ stands to the left, bending right towards the girl, who is lying at the right in a red gown over blue. 8:55 'Taking her by the hand he called, saying/ Child arise . . .'.

45b TRC. Christ casting out a demon. Christ in blue over gold with turban and halo cast out the demon that was dumb from a man kneeling with both hands half outstretched. The text on the right is the passage about Christ teaching his disciples how to pray while the passage immediately below the picture in the right column is 11:14 'Now he was casting out demon . . .'.

46a RBM. Three candles 11:33–34 'No one after lighting a lamp'.

46b LBM. The Holy Spirit 12:12 'for the Holy Spirit will teach you'.

48b (a) LCM. Christ the Shepherd carrying a sheep on his shoulders. Full-frontal figure of Christ with nimbus. 15:5 'And when he has found it, he lays it on his shoulders, rejoicing'.

(b) CLC. Small miniature (3.5 × 2) of the woman sweeping the room for the lost coin. Ten coins strewn on the floor. 15:8 'Or what woman having ten silver coins . . .'.

(c) RTC. A picture of the prodigal son (with no border), in green tunic and red stockings, and holding a crook, drives two pigs to the right. 15:15 'he sent him into his fields to feed swine'.

(d) BRC. The father of the prodigal son standing to the right of the picture outside the gate of his house with an angel behind him embraces his son approaching him from the left with the second angel behind him. 15:20 '. . . and ran and embraced him and kissed him/ 21 'And the son said to him . . .'.

49a BRC. The Rich man and Lazarus. The rich man is represented naked standing with hands outstretched in an enclosure engulfed in fire looking right towards Abraham sitting with 'Lazarus in his bosom'. The two sections of the picture are separated by a large bowl containing water allusion to 'send Lazarus to dip the end of his finger in water and cool my tongue' (16:24). 16:23 '. . . he lifted up his eyes, and saw Abraham far off and Lazarus in his bosom/ 'And he called out' (fol. 49b col. 1).

50b LM. The blind man of Jericho kneeling *18:35–36*

51a RTM. Zacchaeus who has climbed up into a tree 19:4–5 (the relevant text is on fol. 50b col. 1).

52a RBM. The Temple *21:38*

53a TLC. The Betrayal. To the left, a group of soldiers in Crusader tunics, with pikes. Judas in green tunic in the centre facing right, kisses Christ. Three disciples are shown in the bottom corner two asleep and the third looking toward Christ. 22:47 'He drew near to Jesus and kissed him/for he had . . .".

(b) TRC. Peter's denial. The maid, with four soldiers and Peter sit around a fire 'kindled in the middle of the courtyard' while to the right of the picture Jesus is being led by a soldier into the house of the high priest. The moment captured is specified by the text 22:61 'And the Lord turned and looked at Peter'/And Peter remembered the word of the Lord'.

(c) RBM. The full-figure of Peter with nimbus weeping; 'And he went out and wept bitterly' (22:62).

54a BLC. The Crucifixion (6 × 9 cm). Christ on Cross centre, with high beam. His body is slightly bent. St Mary in purple over blue to the left, with right hand outstretched and another woman behind. St John to the right, beardless with head bowed resting in the palm of his hand. The wall of the city forms the background. 23:46 'And having said this he breathed his last/Now when the centurion'.

54b CLC. The Road to Emmaus. Christ to the left of the picture is walking towards the two disciples bent to the right walking. Below green grass, with flowers bent to the right in the breeze. 24:1 'Jesus himself drew near and went with them/'But their eyes were . . .(16)'.

St John

56a Blank
56b Full-page portrait of John with Prochoros.
57a Headpiece of St John's Gospel. Carpet head, with septafoil niche. The arm of the initial letter 'I' has with its framed borders the symbols of the four evangelists one on top of the other starting with an oxen (Luke), the lion (Mark), an angel holding aloft a red book and an open scroll on which are the words in very small miniscules 'Iskzbanē ēr bann' (Matthew). The horizontal arm of the letter 'I' is formed by the looped representation of an eagle. The text of two lines of ornamental letters, 3 lines of uncials, 7 lines of miniscules in various colours are of later hand.
58a LBC. The wedding at Cana. Christ to the left outside the frame of the picture in blue over gold tunic, stretches his hand in blessing over water jars of various shapes and colours which stand at the foot of the picture. To the top right of the frame, the bride and groom sit on a couch under a canopy. 2:7 '. . . with water. And they filled them up to the brim/'He said to them'.
59b LTC. Christ healing the paralytic. The paralytic naked except the loin cloth around his waist sit to the left of the picture with an arm raised faces left towards Jesus who is standing next to a portico which has a large fountain with two waterspouts discharging water. 5:8 'Rise, take up your pallet, and walk'/'And at once the man was healed'.
64a Top, across the page. The Raising of Lazarus (12 × 9 cm). To the left, two disciples in swirling robes (heads missing due to the repair) follow, Christ in the centre, wearing blue over red tunic, approaches right, with swirling garments and right hand outstretched. He is barefoot and bearded. Mary and Martha prostrate below. Four mourners (two old men, one young) stand round the tomb, the lowest carrying the plank of door. To the right, Lazarus standing in white graveclothes, and with beard. The background was gold gilt and the ground is painted green. 11:46 'but some of them went to the Pharisees and told them what Jesus had done'/47 'So the chief priests . . .'.
65a Bottom across page. The washing of the feet. Christ standing to the left, faces right. He is wearing a purple robe, and holds a white towel, below there is a stoup. Disciples to the left in the centre Peter sits, facing left, his feet outstretched into the stoup, and with his right hand to his head. Three other disciples are sitting behind him. 13:16 'Truly, truly, I say to you, a servant is not greater/than his master; nor is he who is sent . . .' (fol. 65b).
65b BLC. The Communion of the Disciples (6.5 × 9.5 cm). Architectural setting of tall narrow building with round-headed arches. Disciples to the left in a group; Christ seated to the right on a raised dais; he is bearded, and wears a blue gown over red. He proffers wafer with the right hand and holds the golden chalice in the left hand. Judas who is receiving the Communion has no halo which distinguishes him from the others who have. 13:26 'So when he had dipped the morsel, he gave it to Judas, the Iscar/27 'Then after the morsel . . .'.
68a CLC. Christ led away to Golgotha, wearing a high crown of thorns, which are blue and purple, and with halo. Two soldiers walk from behind out of the city gates to the right. The gold of the background has held. 19:5 'So Jesus came out, wearing the crown of thorns and the purple robe/He said to them, 'Here is the man'.
(b) BRC. Christ carrying the cross. The procession moves to the right, led on right by a soldier in white helmet, green tunic and red stockings. Christ is clothed in blue over purple and has a halo. He holds the cross in his right hand, leaning out over his right shoulder. Three soldiers at the left follow behind. 19:17 '. . . and he went out, bearing his own cross/to the place called' (fol. 68b).
68b RLC. The Burial of Christ (6 × 9 cm). Above, against a gold background, Joseph of Arimathea and Nicodemus lay Christ bearded and wrapped in white linen into a purple tomb. Below, three women in golden haloes, sitting in mourning (Cf. fol. 23b). 19:38 'So he came and took away his body/39 'Nicodemus also, who had . . .'.

The Revelation to John

70b CLC. Small carpet head in text, serving as headpiece for St John's Revelation. The whole of chapter 22 is wanting.

Or.5761. Yovhannēs of Tarōn, AD 1402

Fol.	*Subject*	*Text*
	St Matthew	
27b	A sheep: 'Behold, I send you out as sheep'	*10:16–17*
33b	Jonah in the belly of the whale	*12:40–41*
38a	John the Baptist's head on a platter placed on the head of a bird	*14:10–13*
52b	The Temple	*20:17–18*
53b	A fig tree	*20:29–30*
55a	A fig tree	*21:18–19*
62a	A temple with two birds resting on the columns	*24:1–2*
73a	An ornate cross with a dove descending on it	*26:56–58*
74a	A cock (in the middle margin)	*26:75*
	St Mark	
113b	A fig tree	*11:12–13*
116a	The Temple	*13:1–3*
120a	The Temple	*14:1–2*
128	A cock	*14:68*
	St Luke	
140a	A shepherd playing the flute and two sheep blowing flames	*2:8–9*
141a	The Temple (Presentation in the Temple)	*2:22–24*
142a	The Temple: 'Now his parents went to Jerusalem'	*2:41–42*
187b	The blind beggar of Jericho	*18:35–36*
189a	A palm tree	*19:29–30*
198a	A cock	*22:60–62*
	St John	
208b	'The lamb of God'	*1:29*
210a	Three jars	*2:7–8*
234a	A palm tree	*12:12–14*
246b	An ornate cross	*19:1–5*

APPENDIX C

Comparative table of the full-page miniatures of the episodes in the life of Christ

Or.2680 Vawray, 1317	Or.2668 Balu, 1437	Or.2707 Bžunikʿ, 1542	Add.7940 Constantinople, 1600?	Or.5737 Isfahan
—	—	7b Vision of Ezekiel (PL. XIII)	—	—
—	—	8b Tree of Jesse (PL. XIV)	—	—
—	—	9b The Annunciation	1b The Annunciation	5a The Annunciation
2b The Nativity (PL. XI)	1b The Nativity	10 The Nativity	2a The Nativity	6a The Nativity
3a Presentation in the Temple	—	11a Presentation in the Temple	3b Presentation in the Temple	4a Presentation in the Temple (PL. XV)
The Baptism of Christ	2b The Baptism of Christ (PL. XX)	12a The Baptism of Christ	4a The Baptism of Christ	7a The Baptism of Christ
3b The Transfiguration	3b The Transfiguration (PL. XXI)	13b The Transfiguration	5b The Transfiguration	8a The Transfiguration
The Raising of Lazarus	—	14a The Raising of Lazarus	6a The Raising of Lazarus	3b The Raising of Lazarus
4a Entry into Jerusalem (PL. XII)	—	15b Entry into Jerusalem	7b Entry into Jerusalem	2a Entry into Jerusalem
4b The Last Supper	—	—	—	—
The Washing of the Feet	—	16a The Washing of the Feet	8a The Washing of the Feet	9a The Washing of the Feet
5b The Betrayal	—	—	9b The Betrayal (PL. XXII)	—
—	—	—	—	—
5a The Crucifixion	4b The Crucifixion	17b The Crucifixion	10a The Crucifixion	10a The Crucifixion
—	—	—	—	—
The Entombment	5b The Entombment (PL. XXI)	—	11b The Entombment	11b The Entombment
—	6b Harrowing of Hell	—	12a Harrowing of Hell	—
—	—	18a The Resurrection	—	11a The Resurrection
—	7b The Ascension	19b The Ascension	13b The Ascension	12b The Ascension
—	—	20a The Assumption of Virgin Mary	—	—
	—			
—	—	21b The Pentecost	14a The Pentecost	13a The Pentecost
—	—	22a Christ in Glory	15b Christ in Glory	—
—	—	—	—	—
—	—	23b The Second Advent	—	14a The Second Advent
—	—	—	16a The Last Judgement	15a The Last Judgement (PL. XVI)
—	—	—	—	—
—	—	—	—	16a Portrait of Christ
—	—	—	—	17a Portrait of the Virgin Mary holding up a pomegranate with both hands

Or.13895 Kaffa, 1658	Or.5449 New Julfa, 1682	Or.14161 Constantinople, 1695	Or.5761 Tarōn, ?	Or.139333 ?
—	—	—	—	—
—	—	—		
4b The Annunciation	1b The Annunciation	1b The Annunciation	—	—
5a The Nativity	2a The Nativity	2a The Nativity	—	—
6b Presentation in the Temple	3b Presentation in the Temple	3b Presentation in the Temple	—	—
7a The Baptism of Christ	4a The Baptism of Christ	4a The Baptism of Christ	—	—
8b The Transfiguration	5b The Transfiguration	5b The Transfiguration	—	—
—	6a The Raising of Lazarus	6a The Raising of Lazarus	—	—
9a Entry into Jerusalem	7b Entry into Jerusalem	7b Entry into Jerusalem	—	—
—	—	8a The Last Supper (PL. XVIIIa)	—	—
—	8a The Washing of the Feet	9b The Washing of the Feet (PL. XVIIIb)	—	—
—	9a The Betrayal	10a The Betrayal		
—	—	11b The Road to Calvary		
10b The Crucifixion	10a The Crucifixion	12a The Crucifixion		121a The Crucifixion
—	11b Descent from the Cross	—		—
—	—	—		—
—	—	—		—
11a The Resurrection	12a The Resurrection	13b The Resurrection		—
12b The Ascension (PL. XIXa)	13b The Ascension	14a The Ascension		—
—	14a The Assumption of Virgin Mary	—		
13a The Pentecost (PL. XIXb)	—	15b The Pentecost		—
—	15b Christ in Glory (PL. XVII)	—		—
14a Christ the Judge	—	—		—
—	—	—		—
15a The Last Judgement	16a The Last Judgement	16a The Last Judgement	1a The Last Judgement	—
—	—	—	—	202b Christ Enthroned
—	—	—	—	—
—	—	—	—	

INDEX